DISSOLVING THE EGO

HELEN HAMILTON

BALBOA.PRESS
A DIVISION OF HAY HOUSE

Balboa Press books may be ordered through booksellers or by contacting:

Balboa Press
A Division of Hay House
1663 Liberty Drive
Bloomington, IN 47403
www.balboapress.co.uk
UK TFN: 0800 0148647 (Toll Free inside the UK)
UK Local: 02036 956325 (+44 20 3695 6325 from outside the UK)

Print information available on the last page.

ISBN: 978-1-9822-8274-5 (sc)
ISBN: 978-1-9822-8273-8 (e)

Balboa Press rev. date: 02/18/2021

DEDICATION

This book is written for all those who wish to be free of suffering. It is dedicated to humanity and to all sentient Beings. It is the wish of the author that it help those ready to live in Freedom. It is humbly offered so that it might light the pathway when things may seem most dark.

Your Liberation is worth pursuing; no effort, struggle or despair will stop you and this book will be your guide. You CAN do it and you would not be reading this if you were not already called. Many are called to wake up but only a few believe they can do it. This book will walk with you to the goal.

CONTENTS

INTRODUCTION

This book is primarily written as an instruction manual. It came as a response to the hundreds of questions from students along the lines of "I know this mentally but how do I live like this?" Over and over again students would have insights and revelations into what they really are. Time and time again a glimpse would be seen that in fact we are not separate people; nor have we ever been. These glimpses came often for many but still there seemed to be little clear instruction on how to dissolve the egoic sense of self. This book is written for that purpose.

It's one thing to see what you are and it is another thing altogether to fully dedicate your life to your total awakening. Few are the ones that have walked all the way to the end of the road and this is due to many factors which we will look into.

What Stops People Awakening?

The first reason most people don't wake up is that they don't have a clear insight into what they actually are. If you are reading this book and have not had a glimpse of what you are, of the Noumenon Itself, it's ok. Throughout the course of applying what you read here you will begin to see the Truth of your Being over and over. This book will help those fastest that HAVE seen and have chosen in their hearts to live from this place of Truth. It is intended for those that find it simply impossible to spend one more day as a separate person because it is no longer tolerable.

Regardless of your experience or knowledge in these matters, this book is for you. It will help you begin from wherever you are starting from and move into total Freedom from the mind.

The second reason we do not usually wake up is because we have believed that it's too hard, it will cost us too much and that losing our sense of being a person will be a huge sacrifice that we will always regret. We can also fear that we will become some kind of automaton or robot with no ability to think for ourselves upon awakening. This is simply not true and this book will help you see that.

The third reason is because we have had very few contemporary examples of awakened Beings in our lives. We have heard of the great Sages and Avatars that lived long ago and we may see living Teachers here now, around us and on YouTube, but deep down in our mind we believe that Enlightenment is only for the lucky few or those that have a superhuman ability to concentrate. We may also believe that we need to have a living Teacher to talk to or that it is impossible to wake up fully in one lifetime. All these myths pervade the human consciousness and stop us from believing in our own liberation.

It is time to make a new paradigm. One in which many of us wake up and it becomes easier and easier for those that follow us because we have been living examples of Truth and the fact it is possible. Never has it been easier to wake up fully out of your limited sense of self into total Peace. Never has there been more help readily available through books like this or over the internet. Everything is set for you to wake up fully and shine as your True Being, but you must believe it is possible for you, even when others may tell you it's not.

You are not being asked to become anything other than you already are. You are only being asked to see clearly and then make a stand for freedom. All you need will come to you to complete the journey and detailed instructions are given in this book to help. Are you ready?

What This Book Will Not Give You

This book will not spend time describing the Enlightened State and what it's like to live the Awakened Way. There has already been plenty of description of this and it serves no purpose to write about that here. Each time it is described it is only more mind food that will be taken, conceptualised and used to continue the dream of being a "someone" alone in time and space. I would like you to find out for yourself what it's like. Become what you have seen and live it fully.

The only thing that will be said about what happens when the ego dissolves finally is that it is totally worth it. It is worth spending every spare minute that you have in practice. It is worth every seeming sacrifice (it is later seen that anything you thought you had to give up was actually worthless anyway) and it is worth it every time you might have to muster up courage to go further.

There is nothing in this world that will compare with the Total Realisation of Truth. We are not discounting this world and all the experiences it has to offer but simply asking you to wake up first and be a beneficial source of Light to the world rather than a drain on it.

Why Do We Use the Word "Noumenon" Rather Than "God"?

Throughout the book there are many names given to what you are, such as Silence, Stillness, Being, Pure Awareness and many more. These are all names for That which has no name and is in no need of a name. It cannot be described in words yet we must use some label for It so that we may point towards It in this text.

We use the word "Noumenon" most often because it has very little (if any) previous meaning to most people. The Buddha avoided the use of the word "God" because for most people this word had so much "baggage" attached to it and so much programming around it. Spiritual students had very little room to explore what was to be found because they had so many preconceived ideas about God. Today's modern spiritual seeker is very well read and educated and is often used to terms such as "True Self", "Pure Awareness", "God", "Enlightenment", "Truth" or "Reality" among many others. It therefore serves us to use a name that has very little previous connections for most people AND accurately describes what it refers to (see the chapter titled: "What is the Noumenon?").

Awakening is really a letting go of all we believe and think to be true and as such we will also have to let go eventually of what we think Reality is and what we think we are. The term "Noumenon" helps us to do that; the meaning it has for you will be developed by you from the inside and not read about, learned or thought about. This is the best gift I can give you — the chance to find out for yourself.

How to Use This Book

It is advised that you read this book in its entirety at least once. Any urge to skip over certain chapters will most likely be resistance coming to the surface. Even though you may feel you are reading the same thing again, know that this is done on purpose; important points are highlighted, repeated and in bold quite often because consciousness learns in a non-linear way. We learn spiritual information by reading or listening to it but we BECOME this information, by absorbing it again and again until it becomes familiar to us. When it becomes familiar it is accepted and acted upon.

Use this book as inspiration to continue along the pathway if you need to. Read and re-read and convince yourself of the importance of taking this journey.

Use this book as an instruction manual for each stage of your journey. Everyone that has ever awoken has had to have instruction from someone who has already completed the journey. It is worth re-reading the book occasionally too in order to see if any habits of resistance or avoidance have subtly crept in.

Reading the book in linear sequence is not necessary but is helpful and recommended. The order of the chapters is designed to cause a shift in consciousness and inspire the desire to fully awaken, if it is not already occurring.

It's possible that someone may read only one chapter, choose one stage one practice and fully awaken without reading another page after applying what they read to all areas of their life completely and without reservation. Most of us are not so driven as yet so you must ignite the fire to fully Realise your True Self by reading and contemplating what you read.

When you think about what you have read you will find a fire is lit within you to BE what you are reading about and it grows stronger each day.

What is written in these words can only represent what you are. Heaven cannot be described in a book but the way to it can be shown clearly. Think of this book as a roadmap and compass and most importantly GET STARTED.

CHAPTER I

What is the Noumenon?

The Noumenon is what you are, but you have been taught to think of yourSelf as a phenomenon.

The Noumenon is a very useful name for what you really are and as such it will always be capitalised in this book. It is useful to look at the classical definition of the Noumenon, and the "opposite" of it which is a phenomenon (plural is phenomena):

Noumenon:

- A thing as it is in itself, as distinct from a thing that is knowable by the senses.
- A thing which is knowable only without the use of ordinary sense perception.
- A thing that cannot be experienced through the senses.

Phenomenon:

- The object of a person's perception
- A fact or situation that is observed to exist
- An event, fact or happening that can be observed to occur.

We can see from these definitions that the Noumenon is something that you cannot experience through the physical senses; we cannot see it, taste it, touch it or smell it. We can also know that the Noumenon is not something that has a finite existence in time, meaning it has no start or ending. We can contrast this with a phenomenon which has a distinct start and end in time and has a duration or lifespan. A phenomenon can be seen, felt, touched or experienced. The Noumenon cannot.

We cannot come to know what we are and live as That by using just the methods that have worked in the past. We have been taught to gather knowledge and to learn about things and to acquire information. We have also been taught to value above all else the tangible world of objects and events; to judge what we can see, feel, hear, taste, touch or think about as real. We have also been conditioned to totally disregard what is invisible, intangible and formless. A good analogy is the moment we enter a room, we immediately look at the objects in the room but totally ignore the space in it or the air in it. If we see a lake or a body of water we immediately look at the birds floating on the surface and not the water. In this way we immediately bypass the obvious Noumenon that is the Silent Field in which all objects and phenomena appear.

Phenomena come and go. The Noumenon Is, always.

Phenomena of Thought

We have a habitual tendency to define ourselves by what we see; we think we are what we see. The first thing most of us notice is a sense of being someone that is made up of the phenomena of thoughts about ourselves. These can be thoughts about our history, our potential future, or dreams, hopes or goals, our desires and much more. We notice immediately this collection of familiar thoughts and we call it "me" and "my mind". We do not stop to notice that these thoughts appear in something that can recognise thoughts but ITSELF IS NOT A THOUGHT.

Thoughts are the first phenomena to appear in the Noumenon. The Noumenon is Silent, Infinite, Still, Peaceful, Invisible, Intangible and beyond time and space and yet all things appear in It. The first thing to appear in it is the thought "I am" or "I exist". After this, a whole lifetime's worth of thoughts are accumulated and we are systematically trained to pay more attention to what appears *in* the Noumenon than *the* Noumenon Itself.

How many times a day do you stop to look at what is looking at your thoughts?

How many times a day do you listen to your listening?

Have you ever wondered what is watching the endless succession of thoughts come and go?

Have you ever wondered why your attention ALWAYS goes to what you are thinking and NEVER goes to what is noticing the thinking?

Even the sense of "me" is not permanent. It was not here last night in deep sleep but it re-emerges every morning to feature throughout the whole waking day, then disappears again as you go to sleep. Even this sense of "me" is a phenomenon appearing in You — the Noumenon.

It does not matter if these are merely words for you right now. In time you will come to live from this place CONSCIOUSLY (you already are the Noumenon but It has not as yet recognised Itself). Apply what you learn in this book and all that will change.

Learn to discriminate between form and formlessness. Learn to discern what is You and what is not you. Thoughts, emotions, perceptions, opinions, events, relationships, sensations and bodies all have a beginning and an ending and as such have to be phenomena and will not stay. Everything you can perceive is not the True You. Even this sense that "I am conscious/awake/aware" is not the True You. Use the tools in this book to take you to the Highest Place and make a stand there.

Change of Values and Habits

In this process we are really only turning around two habits:

Habit 1 — To value phenomena above that which they arise in. To value phenomena as the most important thing (including thoughts!).

Habit 2 — The habit of putting all of our attention on what comes and goes and giving no attention at all to what is Eternal.

Gradually we will turn around these habits by redirecting our attention back to the Noumenon again and again until this becomes the predominant habit. It is as simple as that. As we focus on what we really are, the delusions about ourselves begin to fall away. It is like pricking a hole in a balloon and watching the air begin to leak out. At some point the balloon is lifeless and empty. We simply need to stop the habit of feeding attention to the phenomenon of the egoic sense of "me". This redirection of attention happens gradually over time for most people, but is accelerated by the practices in this book.

You cannot simply stop a habit but you can replace it with another. We can replace the habit of looking at our thoughts, emotions and body and believing we are them. We can begin to put attention on the Noumenon and gradually it becomes more and more clear that this is what we have always been.

You can succeed at turning around these habits because they were not original to you. It takes effort and energy to keep the attention focused on thoughts and it was not easy for you when you were small to learn to do this. Any habit can be turned around with consistent effort and soon you will revert back to your natural state.

The Noumenon is not some far away mystical concept. It is That which hears the inner speech of thoughts and outer speech of words. It is That which sees the inner images in the mind and outer images of the physical world.

The question "What is the Noumenon?" is heard by the Noumenon! This sense of "me" is not what you think it is!

(See the appendix A at the end of the book to help discern the difference between the Noumenon and a phenomenon)

CHAPTER 2

What is the Ego?

The ego is really that part of us that believes that we are a separate being, alone in time and space and trying to make it through life. The ego is not to be judged as wrong or to be alienated in any way even though it seems to be the cause of our suffering. True understanding of what the ego is will immediately begin to dissolve it then we can see it is no longer an enemy to be defeated, but simply the animalistic part of ourselves that allowed us to survive up until this point. Just like the software programme on a computer that is now in need of an upgrade, we can see this sense of being a separate "someone" served us for a while but now we are ready to upgrade.

How Did the Ego Form?

The egoic sense of self is simply an energetic mass of beliefs, conditioning and habits of thought that have taken on a life of their own with the investment of our belief. At first there was only this pure Self that you are then at some point the body appeared in your Awareness. Suddenly, there was a sense of you being inside this body and you began to identify with the body. Over time, as an infant, you began to learn how to make this body do what you wanted it to and gradually you began to forget you were the One operating all bodies. This human body that you had now became the focus of all your attention.

As the body and brain grew and matured, the thoughts about the body and the mind become more and more complex. Conditioning was given to you that this body is what you are and that you are separate from others, from the Self and from Peace. In time, the belief that you are the body grew and became a very strong neuro-pathway in the brain. You began to unconsciously filter out any experiences that were in opposition to this belief and you began to try to accumulate all that you could get to make you feel more secure. Fear replaced peace and tension replaced relaxation as the normal emotions.

As your ability to think about yourself grew and you reached adolescence you began to add to the definition of what you took yourself to be. Along with the body you now believed yourself to be the mind too and so you began to treasure and protect the content of your mind; all the various thoughts that began to emerge were owned as "mine". Opinions, beliefs, desires, goals and dreams that you had all became a part of "me" and so did all your thoughts about your failings, your lack of worth, things that you still need to get and much more. This sense of "me" was now a complex mix and body, mind and belief were in a constant state of need. This need to accumulate things and possessions to feel safe began to expand and you began to try to accumulate intangible things such as self-worth, self-respect, love, appreciation and security.

This is where you stayed for many lifetimes as the bodies came and went. Each time a body appeared, you began to accumulate and struggle in a world which did not seem to ever be able to give you enough to feel complete and safe. If a sense of completion did come it was short lived; perhaps the product of some sporting or academic achievement or as a result of finding the right mate or having children. In time even this too did not satisfy the void that was felt inside. Nothing can satisfy this void because it is the result of the false belief in being a "someone" located inside a body and vulnerable to poverty, disease, adversity and an eventual end when the body dies.

The Dawning of Wisdom

The harder your mind and body tried to find happiness in the world the more elusive it seemed to you. Eventually you began to give up hope and began to question whether this struggle for existence was all there was. Questions began to appear in your mind that had never happened before, such as "what is the point of all this?" and "there must be more to life than this". A doorway was opened in that moment to begin to see the Truth of your Being, that you have never been limited or separate. At some point you encountered a True teacher or teaching and you began to see that perhaps all that was ever "wrong" was that you had mistakenly identified yourself as something that comes and goes - a body and a mind. Now you have drawn to you the means to turn around this belief and to begin to let go of it.

The egoic sense of self is simply a collection of thought patterns in the mind about what we are. They have served us well to allow us to be mature enough as an adult to be able to contemplate what is beyond the egoic sense of self. Now it is time to move beyond. Like an old jacket that no longer fits, we can simply take off the belief of being separate and begin to put more attention on our True Nature as the Infinite One.

How Do We Dissolve the Ego?

We don't necessarily need to make an effort to dissolve the ego because it does not really exist as an actual entity. It is simply a collection of (very) familiar thoughts mixed with attention and investment of belief that they are "mine" or "me". This collective bundle of beliefs about life, ourselves, the world, God, the Universe is what we take ourselves to be and needs constant reinforcement all the time. Note how you can hear people constantly re-affirming their "me-ness" when talking and how it seems more real when you talk about it.

The egoic sense of being a separate someone needs an enormous amount of energy to be fed to it constantly and this has been happening for so long that you have forgotten just how much. As you begin to take attention away from this sense of you, you will begin to feel a more and more effortless state appearing. This perhaps, may be the first taste of the Noumenon. It feels like home, security, completeness and peace.

It may initially take some effort on our part to stay vigilant as we hold attention on what is true about us and refuse the attention going with the thoughts. Attention automatically will go with thoughts if we do not stay observant.

We must simply keep attention on the Noumenon by using one of the practices in Stage One. We can then allow the egoic sense of "me" to dissolve just like an old ruined building will immediately begin to collapse if we stop running around constantly propping it up. What is false falls away once seen to be false and we need not do anything to make that happen.

We are the Self believing ourselves to be the separate sense of self. We must make use of this separate sense of self whilst it is here. It is in fact the reason for having this complex human brain that is capable of contemplating itself and this ability is present in no other species except humanity. We must learn to use this sense of self to focus consistently and only on the Self. We must use the practices in Stage One, Two and Three to focus on the True Self like a laser beam and this begins to burn away all delusion and illusion about our True Nature.

This Awareness that we are has the ability to focus on something when it flows through this body. Use this focusing ability like a lighthouse that can light the Truth of your Being. This small self has been focused consistently on the world outside and on the objects of our sense perception. This gave us the illusion of being someone viewing the world out there and having an independent, separate existence from it. As we turn attention around 180 degrees onto that Self that is looking at Itself, we begin to allow the Truth to reveal Itself to us.

The Noumenon cannot reveal Itself to us when we are more interested in what is "out there". Everything we think we see is really appearing "in here" in our mind. Focus the self on the Self and hold attention there as is described in Stage One and all your problems will begin to disappear.

Why Do We Want to Dissolve the Ego?

As long as we feel deep down that we are separate from God, from what we want, from life, from others around us or from even the Noumenon, we will always act from a basis of lack, fear and survival. Inherent in the sense of being separate is lack and fear. We will always believe ourselves to be the one trying to get back to God or find our way home. Whether we believe we need outer tangible things or inner intangible things we will always be constantly driven with no rest inside. We will always be trying to accumulate knowledge, power, wealth, friends, love, security and whatever else we think we need to be happy and safe.

As spiritual students, we can spend MANY lifetimes driven by the search for freedom, always believing it to be something "out there" or some state or place we can reach and finally be home. We will always be looking for ourselves by doing some work to get there, all the while missing the essential point that we are already what we are searching for but we have not recognised ourselves.

When the ego dissolves it leaves only the realisation that everything was always perfect and complete and that there never could have been any lack. Even once you have started the process in earnest you will begin to notice more clarity, peace, a sense of growing freedom and that nothing ever was wrong in the first place.

The egoic sense of self was needed to ensure the survival of the human species but now it is time to let go of all limiting self-definitions and wake up fully to the Truth of your Being. You are the Noumenon watching another human experience and once you know this, then you will live in Peace.

The only way to live in this True Reality is to be willing to see where you have still believed yourSelf to be something limited and finite. If you are willing to see this then it will dissolve and you are free. Enjoy the human experience without any fear. Take in all that human life has to offer and know that what you are cannot end. Live this life in this body fully and embrace every experience, but from your True Place of being the Infinite One.

CHAPTER 3

Benefits of This Pathway

This is a direct path that lights the way to Truth through experience. Nobody can tell you what it's like to live in and as the Noumenon, but they can point out how to experience it. Once you have experienced for yourSelf what you REALLY are, then nobody can say anything that will change that experience. There are many books that describe the Noumenon and it is fine to read and learn about it at first but if your heart is truly longing for freedom, then you must experience the Truth of your Being as soon as possible.

The aim of the instructions in this book is to get you to experience for yourSelf what you are; perhaps for the first time. Once your mind begins to taste the Noumenon even a little it will want more. It will decide it is the most delicious experience we can have! In this way we can win the battle with the mind without fighting because your mind will *want* to engage in practice. Allowing yourSelf to experience what you really are and to fall in love with this totally will allow resistance to melt away.

This book will help you to get to know who you are and get used to feeling the peace, love and joy that is your Natural State. As you get used to feeling this and allow yourSelf to bathe in the light of your Truth as often as you can, then a slow, gradual dissolution of the ego will occur and you can simply watch it happen.

In all pathways the mind must eventually admit that it does not know what you really are and must also admit that it does not know the way to liberation. In this pathway it can be much easier to get to this place because your mind will be more ready to accept the Noumenon having had a taste of it and seeing that it is simply what has always been here. The mind naturally fears the True Being because it does not know what it is and never will. This letting go or leap into the Unknown is hard for many people and they never make it successfully. Many fall at this point. The major benefit of this pathway is that the mind has been introduced to the True Being/Self well before it has to surrender and usually it has been exposed to it many times. The Noumenon almost becomes like a companion or helpful friend to the mind and the mind begins to allow itself to be disarmed.

Dealing with Fear

On any pathway, it is likely that fear about letting go fully into the Truth will arise at some point, but here this will be greatly diminished because you will have seen what you are. If you have read this book and followed the instructions carefully you will have all the tools you need to allow this process of awakening to occur as quickly and easily as possible. Everyone will be tested along the pathway but here you will always have easy and simple instructions to help you in those difficult times.

As you walk the pathway know that every enlightened Sage that ever walked the planet is with you. Every Saint is for you. Every Master is beside you. All those that have done it are supporting you in unseen ways and Grace is helping you as you make each step. Know that you do not need to know how to get through the next challenge; help is here for the asking. It can come in an infinite number of ways.

Devote yourSelf only to Truth, to God, to the Self. Your heart should beat only to see the Truth in everything and everyone you see. Then you will live in the Kingdom of Heaven.

This Experience Will Be Only Yours

This book intentionally makes very little, if any, reference to Sages of the past and traditional teachings or styles of religion in the hope that as such, what you discover will not be tainted or coloured in any way by what you have read, learned or studied spiritually up till now. The modern spiritual seeker has read many books, attended seminars and learnt many styles of meditation and this acquired knowledge can be projected by the mind onto what is read here. It is the aim of this book to be like a blank slate for those that have read and learnt much about awakening but as yet have not been able to put it into practice and turn it from purely theoretical and mental knowledge to a lived experience of Oneness.

This is not meant to invalidate the famous Teachings and Teachers of past and present but to merely guard against the mind's tendency to take information and compare it to what it already knows rather than applying it. This is also a reason why we use the word "Noumenon" to describe what you are rather than a more traditional term.

CHAPTER 4

Stage One Practice:
Learning to Tune In

All of us have had years of practice (lifetimes even) learning to focus attention on the phenomena of thoughts, feelings, and outer events. We all have attachments, patterns we use to distract ourselves, self-sabotaging thoughts and other programming that has been running us. For these reasons we need to devote some time each day to true meditation. This is a simple practice of "no-practice". This is a non-doing practice which means that we are not trying to get anywhere, to achieve any particular state or become something other than we already are. On the contrary, we will begin to tune in to what we already are. Our True Being is Silent, Still, Aware, Awake and is reading this right now. As we learn to give time and attention to the Noumenon we are simultaneously de-programming ourselves away from this constant fixation with the content of the mind and its convictions that we are a separate being trying to find our way home.

We cannot force the mind to be silent, but we can focus on the Silence that is already here in and amongst thoughts. Simply by taking attention away from our mind and putting it on what we really are we begin to de-energise the mind. At some point the mind becomes totally silent all by itself, but before that even happens you will not care whether it's noisy or not.

In this practice we will be learning to tune in to the Noumenon. Now it may sound strange that you have to learn to tune in to what you really are but all of us have had significant programming that tells us thoughts are more important than what we actually are. We all have egos that believe firmly that our sense of being someone separate is all we are and that giving this up will result in the end of our existence. The ego holds on tenaciously to this belief and it has no evidence to counter it. As we learn to notice again and again the Silent, Still Field of Awareness that is just Being, then gradually the ego will begin to let go by itself. Simply paying attention to what we are already is enough; you cannot force a letting go to happen but you can show the ego that it is safe to do so. As you learn to tune into the Noumenon, by whichever name you call it, you will find it becomes increasingly irrelevant whether your mind lets go or not, is silent or not.

Tuning In

I want you to think of this practice as if you were tuning in a portable radio so that it can pick up a radio station that's already being broadcast. Learning to pay attention to yourSelf is like that too. You do not need to do anything to make the broadcast happen and to listen to the Silent Field. You simply need to know how to tune in.

The Noumenon is beyond time and space, infinite in its capacity. It is omnipresent and available at all times in all places. There is nowhere that it is not present and that includes you, right here and now. Knowing that the Noumenon MUST be here now allows you to simply relax and begin to tune in. It does not even need to be searched for but simply noticed. Just like if you were listening to loud music and suddenly it stopped. Immediately the silence is noticeable in the absence of noise. The Noumenon is that which is apparent in the absence of all things/phenomena. You do not have to get rid of all thoughts to notice the Noumenon; it is enough to simply see that thoughts are appearing in this vast field of Awareness that you are. Something is hearing your thoughts — what is it? The Silent Noumenon is always listening, open, aware and observing in an impartial way to all that is occurring in it.

Relaxing and listening is the way. Knowing it is here and feeling for it is key. You do not need to exert any effort or strain to find the Noumenon — it has been precisely this effort that has seemingly hidden it from you.

How much effort must you make to be what you already are? How hard will it be to find what is always here all the time and in all places?

The Different Practices

The following section of the book lists many ways to tune into the Noumenon. I suggest you read them all and feel for which one pulls at you. Perhaps one or two of them will be attractive for you. If you are more mind-based then being aware of Awareness may be for you. If you are naturally quite sensual then listening for the Silence may work for you.

As you read the sections, note down which ones feel right or easier to you and give them a try. They are all describing the same practice, a non-doingness. A letting go of effort and tuning in. Right where you are already the Noumenon is here.

The Difference Between the
Inner and Outer Search

Notice that when we are asked to look for something we immediately begin to look outside of ourselves. We usually straight away go to anything that feels like "otherness" such as our thoughts, feelings, world, events, relationships and even our definition of ourselves. The aim of this book is to show you that you have been looking "out there" to find yourself and have not been putting any attention at all on **what** is looking. Could it be simply that what you have always called "me" IS the Noumenon and you simply overlook it every time?

If you follow any one of the practices listed in stage one you will begin to see they are all training you to develop the ability to one-pointedly focus on "in here". Tuning in you will see that what is already here is the biggest prize you could ever ask for AND is in fact what you have been searching for. We have been programmed, taught and trained to look "out there" and to totally ignore what is doing the looking.

Note that even the "inner world" of thoughts, feelings, sensations and emotions is "out there" to the Noumenon. Even this subtle inner world of thoughts, opinions, mind in general and our sense of self is "out there" to what you really are. Doesn't it stand to reason that you must be here before you can even notice a thought?

The outer search is a reaching, trying, becoming, wanting, trying to find, hoping to achieve or reaching a destination type of search. It involves a tremendous amount of effort and will not succeed.

The Inner Search is a relaxation, a tuning into, a clarity of focus, a final seeing, an understanding, a re-contextualisation,

a softening and inclusion, an allowing and a letting it be as it is. It is effortless and immediately bears fruit.

Resistance

If you cannot find or choose one of the practices, or none of them feel right to you, then it is very likely that your mind is putting up strong resistance. Tell your mind that it is ok and nobody is going to do anything to it. Our mind will fear what is new to it but it will come to see that tuning in to the Noumenon feels relaxing and is calming. In time the practice will begin to cause a deeper happiness and peace and your mind will want to tune in.

Every awakened Sage has had to push through this resistance and do it anyway. So can you.

A Few Notes

You are not becoming anything with this practice.

You are not looking to achieve a particular state.

You are not trying to silence your mind — merely to find the Silence that is here already despite the thoughts.

You are not trying to leave your body or do any kind of spiritual acrobatics.

You are simply sitting and tuning in; like sitting down with an old friend and listening to what they have to say.

You are not trying to get anywhere.

You are not trying to achieve anything.

You are simply sitting to notice what is already here but has been overlooked till now.

You are not trying to manipulate the Noumenon.

You don't have to have a quiet mind for this to work.

You do not need to be an expert meditator. Forget all you already know about meditation.

There is no end result we are looking for here. It is enough to tune in to the Noumenon.

CHAPTER 5

Being Aware of Awareness

At every moment we are aware; we can begin to see that there is always Awareness present. Something within us is always seeing. We have been trained to focus our Awareness totally on what we are aware OF and not at all on the Awareness itself.

All day throughout the waking hours we are aware of thoughts, emotions, social interactions, our body, events in the world and on it goes. There is a background of Awareness that is always noticing whatever is going on in the outer world such as where our body is, who we are with, what the weather is like etc. It is also always noticing what is going on in our inner world of thoughts, feelings and sensations in the body.

This Awareness is not some far off place that you have to reach; on the contrary. It is so common and normal to you that you do not ever notice it! Every time you say "My mind is so busy" then you are noticing what your mind is doing but putting no attention on that which notices. **The practice is simply to take your attention away from what you are aware OF and to put it on the Awareness itself.**

21

Helen Hamilton

Awareness is not a feeling and does not feel any particular way. It is just aware. Every time you say "I know" it is this same Awareness recording all that is appearing in front if of it but you call it "me". It is simply that aware intelligence that seems to wake up every morning and watches all that occurs each day until the time comes for sleep. It is not special and it will not feel special; it just is. Awareness is just the ordinary Awareness that you are using right now to read this. If somebody came in the room and began to talk to you then you would effortlessly be aware of that person and what they were saying. You cannot switch off Awareness.

The Practice of Being Aware of Awareness

At first it is enough to simply set aside some time each day to sit down and be aware that you are aware. It is as simple as noticing that you have Awareness. At any moment you cannot deny you are aware because you are aware of all the stimuli coming in through the senses.

Simply being aware of your Awareness is enough. You can only be aware of Awareness or aware of your thoughts but not both at the same time. Frequently you will notice Awareness has gone to thoughts and you must simply redirect your Awareness back to being aware of itself. Awareness aware of Awareness. That simple. No tricks.

Thinking about being aware is NOT the same as simply being aware of Awareness. This will be your mind's biggest trick to stop you practising and so you must overcome this and see it clearly. Any thought about Awareness is noticed in the Awareness itself. We have all spent much time thinking about Awareness and that has not worked. This is probably one of the reasons you were drawn to this book, to finally move beyond this. Thinking about something and the actuality of it

22

are very different things. Thinking about Awareness leads to a stronger sense of separation. Being aware of Awareness will begin to dissolve the separateness. It is either one or the other.

You can only be aware of one thing at once so you are either aware of your Awareness or not.

The Progression of the Practice

As you start your practice, it will feel like there is a sense of "I am aware of my Awareness". As if there are two entities in fact. It will feel as though there is a "you" which is aware of the bigger Awareness. Everyone must start from here and this is ok.

As you continue your practice, it will be realised at some point as a *knowing* (rather than a thought) that Awareness is simply aware of itself. It will be seen clearly that Awareness is simply choosing to focus on itself rather than any other supposed object "out there" and this includes thoughts. Thoughts are "out there" to the pure Awareness that you are.

As you progress you will see that Awareness is developing more and more of a taste for itself and has less interest in what it is aware OF. To be aware OF something (like thoughts, feelings, objects etc) there must be two things: one thing that is aware and another thing that it is aware of. We could say that being aware of something is where the split into two seeming entities occurred — a "me" that is trying to get back to the Self.

This does not mean that you'll become unable to function in the world or hold a conversation as you cannot be aware of where your body is or what someone is saying; it is more that you will be aware of everything in your field of experience without any tendency to label them with names and forms. You simply begin to take it all in panoramically.

As with each one of these practices, at first you will need to make time to sit down and be aware of your Awareness but as you continue you will begin to notice you are aware of Awareness when you are moving around your life. An example of this is that you might suddenly see that when you are driving, Awareness must be aware to be able to watch the road and you are noticing it. You might find yourself listening to someone talk and suddenly understand that Awareness must be there to hear the words and as soon as you realise this, Awareness is aware of Itself.

Notice the tendency of mind to object by saying "I cannot be aware of Awareness when I am doing something else." At first, this may seem to be very true. But as you persist, you will see that Awareness can be focused "in here" and "out there" at the same time. In actuality we begin to see that Awareness really does not make a distinction between "in here" and "out there". It only sees the Oneness of Awareness. "In here" and "out there" are simply divisions that have seemed to be very real because we've spent much time reinforcing that belief with thoughts.

Eventually you will see that you are able to be aware of Awareness no matter what the body is doing or the mind is thinking. It will be realised that mind and body are simply happening in your experience and you have a choice always what to be aware of. You will not lose your life, your experiences or your joy by focusing Awareness on itself all the time, but simply you will lose the ability to feel fear and a sense of separation which leads to desire and suffering.

The thought "I am aware" will be seen to be arising in Awareness. The sense of you being aware will be seen clearly to be arising AFTER Awareness is there. You will come to know that Awareness must be there FIRST before any "I" thought can be noticed.

Summary of the Practice

Set aside some time each day to sit down (in any position) and be aware of Awareness. This is as simple as noticing that there is Awareness ALREADY present. As soon as your Awareness becomes aware of thoughts and pays attention to them, you must bring Awareness back to looking at Awareness.

Each time Awareness begins to look at thoughts, emotions and distractions, you must bring it back to being aware of Awareness only. Repeat this for as long as the practice session continues.

In the end it will be seen that there IS only Awareness and nothing else actually exists. All that arises from this Awareness (such as thoughts, a sense of "me") is in fact Awareness simply appearing AS something and not actually a "something". How can anything that arises from this Awareness be anything other than Awareness? Steam that rises from hot water is still water.

Resistance to the Practice

The biggest resistance to the practice may come because you notice there are times when you feel you are unaware of the Awareness and lost in thoughts. Perhaps at first there may be long periods of time where this seems to be the case.

You can overcome this objection by seeing that you are always aware and sometimes you are aware of the feeling or sense of being unaware. This sense of being blocked or unaware has appeared in front of you and your Awareness is noticing it. Remove attention from the "I am not aware" feeling and bring it back to the fact that you can see or notice this feeling. Awareness is always on like the eyes are always seeing. You may walk into a dark room and say "I cannot see anything" and you may believe this; just like your mind will say "I am not aware all the time and I cannot be aware of Awareness when something big comes in front of me like fear." It is more truthful to say that "I can see total darkness in front of me" or in the case of this practice "I am aware of the feeling of being unaware".

Once you realise this you will see that you can never be unaware. Even at night time while the body sleeps you will begin to notice that there is Awareness of the mind being unaware or being asleep.

If resistance continues, re-read the chapter on "Self-Inquiry" and the chapter on "Short Cut" and apply them. Ask yourself what is aware of this resistance and is IT affected by the resistance?

Awareness is not the thought "I am aware". It is That in which all thoughts arise and merge back into. It is here before any thought arises to notice it arise. Therefore no thought can block it in any way.

CHAPTER 6

Listening to the Silence

In the background there is constant Silence that most of us do not hear because we are so focused on the noise of thought, emotion and verbal chatter. Even when we are silent it is usually only because we are being entertained by the television, radio, social media or a number of other things.

In this practice we begin to tune into the Silence that is our Being. Being is just silently being, not doing. It can help us to realise that we can only hear and recognise sound, speech and other noises because it appears against a constant background of Silence. We can only recognise that something has appeared when it appears against a background of something continuous. Similarly, we can only recognise that a sound has stopped because the Silence is there and listening. We get a sense of this when a car or house alarm has been sounding for some time and finally stops; or when a pneumatic drill goes off by our house or we are passed by an emergency ambulance with its sirens blazing. In the sudden absence of the loud noise we can feel a tangible sense of Silence and it can even seem loud.

Silence does not listen in an active way; it is not interested in a personal way in what it hears. We could say that it is openly and lovingly listening to whatever arises in it; it has no opinion about any sound, it hears opinionated thoughts about what it is hearing too!

The Practice of Listening to Silence

Silence is more a way of being than a doing; naturally our being is silent and it can help us to begin to perceive the Silence by just being willing to sit and listen. That's all — just to listen and not to expect to hear anything in particular. Right now we are already hearing the Silence of Being but we have been trained and attuned to habitually pay more attention (or all our attention!) to the noises and sounds that appear than the Silence itself.

It is useful to set aside some time each day where you can sit alone and listen to the Silence. It need not be a long time at all, start from where you are at and whatever you can do. You can even listen to the Silence in the bath or sitting alone with a cup of tea on a morning. There is not any special position to sit in or any other thing to happen other than the fact that you are willing to put your phone on silent and turn off the TV for ten minutes or whatever time you're comfortable with.

In the beginning, it can help to sound a gong or ring a bell. As the noise of the gong or bell fades, we can gradually notice a more palpable feeling of Silence replacing it. In fact it is not replacing it. It's just merely that we are noticing it now. If our Being is the Noumenon, it MUST be here already and everywhere. It must be ever-present as the space in which all else is occurring. All that is occurring is that we are replacing the habit of our attention always going to the phenomena of thought, mind patterns, emotions, sensations and the outer world. We are training our attention to notice the unchanging Silence of the Noumenon first rather than the constantly changing sound phenomena. Thoughts are simply sounds that are heard in our head and we then chose to verbalise them as outer sounds or not.

At first when we begin to tune into the Silence it may feel like nothing at all is happening. We may only notice an absence of sound. We have to be spiritually mature to continue our practice through this phase. We can reach this maturity quickly by seeing it is our mind that is looking for a one off "aha" moment and wants to say "that's it, I have done that practice — what's next?" We are not listening to the Silence to get an effect or achieve an outcome; we are simply attuning ourselves to listen to the Silence for the pure joy it brings.

Whether we notice the Silence or not is actually unimportant. The real spiritual growth comes from the commitment to being willing to sit and listen for even a few moments. This is something most humans will never achieve in a whole lifetime! Of course they cannot be blamed for that as it is simply where they are at. You are different; you have already had enough of the noise of the mind or else you would not be reading a book like this. So persist in your practice and let go of wanting a tangible result. You need no results to be what you are.

The Progression of the Practice

At first it may feel like you are achieving very little and you will have the feeling that "I am listening to the Silence". It will begin to feel perhaps a little relaxing to just sit and listen with no expectations of what you might hear. As time progresses you will begin to notice a sensation of more openness in the body the longer you spend listening to the Silence.

There will probably be the feeling that you can only hear the Silence at first when you are in a quiet room and in formal

29

meditation practice or alone and this is normal and to be expected. As you persist you will begin to spontaneously hear the Silence in other places and in situations where your mind is not so busy, such as when driving or watching a movie. Eventually you will come to notice that the Silence is always here and you can hear it all the time. It is different for each person how long this takes and it should not matter anyway because you will begin to find that you are listening for the Silence simply because of the spacious feeling and quietness that noticing it connects you to.

There will seem to be various stages in your practice and at first it will seem to be only formal practise periods where you make an effort to sit down and shut out the noise and distractions. This is how it will be for a while. Gradually then you will notice yourself spontaneously being aware of Silence even whilst busy in normal activities in life. Practise will move from only formal practise to more and more informal and spontaneous listening. Eventually formal practise will seem to disappear as the one listening begins to be seen as just a thought appearing in the Silence.

As you progress in your practice, you will notice the thought more and more of "I am listening to the Silence" being replaced by a knowing that **you are the Silence Itself listening to Itself**. We could say that the "I am listening to Silence" thought can only be heard in the mind because it appears against a background of Silence. Notice that all that is happening is the Silence is beginning to recognise Itself as Silence and the "I" thought is being heard in That.

Eventually, all that arises out of this Silent Field of Being will be known to also be the Silence too; no matter how noisy it may seem. Just as steam that rises from the surface of hot water cannot be other than water; so too all noises and sound that arise from the Silence must also be made of this Silence and have it as their core.

In the end all sound will only serve to reinforce that you are in fact the Silence of Being and in fact that which knows the Silence. That which knows Silence IS the Silence. A sound cannot recognise the Silence but the Silence can recognise the sound.

Summary of the Practice

Take as much time as you are able each day to listen to the Silence and each time the attention goes back to the noise of thoughts simply bring the attention back to that Silent space which gives birth to all sound. Bring attention back over and over again. That is the practice.

When you feel ready or when it begins to happen by itself, then you can begin to listen for the Silence when you are not formally sitting. This should not replace your formal practice but should add to it and eventually overtake it. Formal practice will fall away as the practiser disappears but this will happen by itself. It is not something you need to decide yourself. Simply set aside some time each day and allow the joy you begin to feel to pull you in deeper and deeper.

Resistance to the Practice

Any time you feel strong resistance to the practice then look at why you feel this is significant. Notice this resistant feeling is appearing in the Silence itself. Notice that if the Silence was not present you could not even hear the "I don't want to do this" thought arise.

If resistance continues or if the thought persists that "I cannot hear the Silence for all the noise in my mind" then re-read the "Self- Inquiry" and "Short cut" chapters and apply them. Ask yourself "where is the sense of 'me' that cannot stay focused and cannot hear the Silence" and see if you can find it. This is a rhetorical question. Disregard all mind answers and stay with the question.

Silence is not a thought. It is That from which thoughts arise and merge back into. No thought can block the Silence or stop you from listening to it.

CHAPTER 7

Resting in the Stillness

When we pay attention to what we are we can notice that our essential nature is Stillness itself. At first this seems to be covered up by the movement that arises out of the Stillness. Movements of thoughts, emotions, perceptions and sensations in our body can seem to be like waves on the surface of the ocean of our Being. We must begin to pay more attention to that within us that can notice the movement or constantly changing content of the mind.

The coming and going of thoughts and feelings is only noticeable to us in contrast, because we are watching it from a place that is totally still and silent. This Stillness is not simply the absence of movement but it is in fact the Noumenon that has never moved. Consider the Noumenon is omnipresent and exists outside of time. How could it move anywhere? It must be by nature inherently still. The Stillness watches all movement that appears within it but is Itself unmoving. For it to move there would have to be some "other" place where it is not so that it could move there.

Something within you is just being; not being anything in particular and not seeking anything. It is not trying to control, to accept, to transcend or to let go of anything. It is not trying to become anything other than it is already. We can get a taste of this Stillness when we see that we are called "human beings" — the human part is something we are very aware of and know well. It is time to get in touch with the Being that simply IS.

We can easily miss this Stillness because it is not shouting for attention or trying to achieve anything. We must become more interested in what is unchanging within us. All things come and go but what we truly are is unchanging and totally still. When we begin to "tune in" to this Stillness that we are it can feel as if a soft relaxing field of energy is descending upon us but it is really that we are beginning to notice the Stillness that has always been here but has been overlooked till now.

The Practice of Resting in the Stillness

Stillness is everywhere and is our essential nature but most of us have a very well developed sense of being someone; of being an individual. We must begin to want to notice that which is not moving and this is easily done when we have had enough of the constant coming and going of the mind. When we know ourselves to be the Stillness and not a "someone" moving around in the Stillness then we are looking from a stable place. When we find ourselves to not only be aware of the Stillness but to actually be it then we are undisturbed by the movement of the mind.

Most of us spend our entire lives trying to make our mind be still; which is really like trying to make something that is always in motion stand still. It is possible to do this but only for short periods of time and usually even if we can still our mind for a short period it will begin to move again soon afterwards and usually be even more chaotic than before.

It is much more effective to put attention on the Stillness that has always been here and then we begin to be less and less affected by the changeful sense of self and the world. We cannot make our mind be still but we can become more interested in the Stillness that is ever present and that is all we need to do.

The Progression of the Practice

When we first begin to practice, it can seem like there is a sense of "I am resting in the Stillness" and we can begin to feel (as with all the practices) a sense of relaxation or heaviness in the body as it begins to respond to the Stillness. It will seem as if you are "tuning into" or "taking a bath" in the Stillness and seem to come in and out of it. In reality what is happening is that for some time each day, we sit and notice the Stillness so we feel it in our body. Then as we end our session and return to our activities, attention goes back to the moving changeful mind by habit. It can seem in this way that the Stillness has gone, when in fact we are simply focused on the movement instead. Stillness is still by its very nature and cannot come or go; it is simply our wandering attention that moves from Stillness to thought.

As we progress in our practice it will be understood at some point that the sense of "me" that seems to be resting in the Stillness is actually only knowable because we are seeing it from the place of total Stillness. What we are looking at is really where we are looking from also. The sense of self will be seen to be a movement simply arising from the Stillness Itself. Stillness will be seen to be no longer appearing to move at all but simply changing appearance.

Summary of the Practice

Begin by setting aside some time each day to sit down and notice the Stillness. As with all the practices, we can begin with however much time we have available but it's better to practice consistently each day than for four hours one day and then miss five days. As you begin to notice the Stillness you will begin to really look forward to your practice session, and eventually your mind will begin to fall in love with the Stillness.

As with the other practices, you will begin to notice that you seem to become aware of the Stillness at other times, when not formally meditating. This is simply that you are becoming aware that the Stillness is always present. At first it is easier to notice it after strenuous movement or activity of the body, after a day's work or first thing in the morning; but eventually you can "find" it every time you choose to tune into it no matter where you are or what you are doing.

At some point it will be seen that the Stillness is ever-present but simply seems to be covered up by focusing on something else. The sense of Stillness being stronger or weaker will fade as it is seen to be only our attention on it that fades. Gradually we come to see we are indeed the Stillness Itself in which our sense of self seems to be moving and having a life of its own. In the end it is seen that no matter what the "me" is doing, we are and have always been the Stillness and as such are indestructible and not subject to anything such as death and birth and all fear disappears.

Resistance to the Practice

Sometimes when you sit down to practice, the sense of the Stillness may seem very present or it may seem to come to the forefront. Sometimes it may even come unasked for. At other times you may feel your mind is too restless to feel the Stillness or that you cannot focus enough on it. At such times it's useful to read and apply the Self-Inquiry chapter. Try to find this sense of "me" within your being that cannot focus. Where actually is this "me" that cannot meditate right now? Search yourself and see if you can find an object. The very looking will begin to dissolve the excess noise and movement that seemingly blocks your ability to notice the Stillness.

Also, whenever you feel the urge read the "Short Cut" chapter and apply it.

Stillness is not the absence of movement of thought; it is That in which thought arises. It is That which has NEVER moved because it is in all places at all times.

CHAPTER 8

Noticing the Sense of Being

Each moment we can look at our mind and see that it is always trying to get somewhere or become something. In the usual state of mind there is always an intention to get more of something, to get rid of something, to sustain a nice experience or to be free of an unpleasant one. When we are mature enough in our pathway, we can see that what we call mind is really just a constant stream of commentary on how things are and how things should be. Our mind is not able to see the perfection that is already here and as such is always chasing some imaginary perfect end point in which we live in peace. For us to reach this imaginary end point, our mind is looking for the perfect set of circumstances when it can finally let go of needing to change anything.

Anytime we hold an intention in our mind it causes a subtle tension within us that is really an energetic attitude that "everything is not all right just as it is". Our mind or sense of being something or someone is always trying to become more, greater, freer, lighter and on and on it goes. No matter what temporary state we may achieve we will always want more.

There is something however that is not trying, doing, becoming, reaching or wanting. It does not need, desire, transcend or let go of anything. We can begin to notice that our human mind is always trying to get or get rid of something and yet our "Beingness" is just being. It is perfectly and effortlessly just Being. Not being someone — just Being. It is not even being peaceful — it is just being. It just IS. It just exists and it is perfect. It's not even concerned with being perfect or trying to be more perfect as it has no ideas or preconceptions. It is not in argument with Reality at all. It IS Reality. Mind is a movement against how things are; a rejection of what already is manifesting in some way.

We can begin to get a taste of this effortless Being that is our true nature when we see that every intention or desire we have is really a denial of what is already here. In seeing this deeply we can begin to let go of intentions and allow what is already here to begin to reveal itself. We must go beyond the common objection in our mind that to let go of wanting something to change means it will not come. In truth the opposite is true; the sooner we let things be as they are, the sooner what we desire can come to pass. Holding onto desire and intention means that we are resisting the fact that what we want is already here and we cannot allow it to manifest into our experience.

The Practice of Noticing the Sense of Being

Each day set aside as much time as you can to simply sit and let go of all intentions to change how things are right now. When it comes to meditation or practice we usually have had a lot of conditioning that we are trying to achieve some positive state and so we can notice an intention arising to feel better or to have a quieter mind and simply let it go.

As we sit quietly *without any intention to change things or to have any particular experience* we will begin to feel a sense of relaxation that deepens into a peaceful state as we progress.

By letting go of wanting peace we begin to see that it is already here. It will be seen in time that all our attempts to get something simply clouds our awareness of what is already here.

At first, it may take a conscious noticing that we are trying to get somewhere or that there is tension in the mind and body and to let it be as it is. As soon as we totally allow ourselves to simply be as we are in this moment, there will be a relaxation occurring in the mind and body. Mind may always be trying to resist what is happening but we do not have to resist that resistance. We can simply make the higher choice to let it be. If there is a wish for the mind to be quiet, we can note that it is there, acknowledge it and fully allow it to be. It is natural and normal for us to want to end suffering and have peace but we must realise that fighting a noisy mind is only going to make it worse. That would be mind fighting mind. As the Beingness itself we can simply BE and make no effort to control whatever is occurring. We can become indifferent to whatever is going on in our mind and simply observe. Observing is passive and by its very nature allowing.

We simply let whatever is happening happen. We are acknowledging that how it is right now is how it is and nothing we can do will change how life has already shown up for us in this moment. We just *BE* with no intention to *DO* anything about our state. Each time that we notice attention has gone back to thoughts and to trying to change something about our experience, we can simply drop it and rest in the Beingness itself AS Being.

Note that we are "human Beings" and not "human doings". To be is enough, the rest happens by itself. Thoughts will come and go, intentions will come and go, emotions will come and go and we can simply stay only as the Beingness that is just watching. Intentions and desires and goals are of the mind and you are not the mind; you know this because you can observe it.

The Progression of the Practice

At first the practice will feel like "I am just Being and letting go of intention". It will feel as if you are dropping everything you are carrying and resting in the Beingness. As time passes and you become more accomplished in the practice, you will begin to see that it is the Beingness that has always been observing and this Beingness is what you are. You are the Beingness that is finally being itself. It is finally able to stop imagining itself as this "me" entity that is managing its life and doing all these actions and is the thinker of thoughts. It will be seen by you that thoughts, actions, emotions and events all simply arise out of You - the Beingness.

In the end you will come to know that there is only this Beingness. That all thoughts and emotions and seemingly solid objects are made of this effortless Being and as such are the same in essence. Everything is happening by itself with no cause of anything. What seems to be manifestation occurring is simply Beingness appearing in different and unique ways. We simply watch the unfolding occur.

Summary of the Practice

Each day take some time to simply sit and be. That means to do nothing, to sit in a comfy position and simply be. You will begin to notice gradually that part of you that is just Being and is not trying to do. It is enough that you notice this Beingness and rest in that AS that. Each time you notice that you have begun to get caught up in thought, simply return your attention to the effortless nature of your Being that is simply perfect as it is. Redirect attention back to the Being over and over as many times as it takes in the practice session.

Resistance to the Practice

Resistance to simply Being may occur as your mind tries to tell you that just observing and Being is irresponsible. It may also feel like you are letting go of control and this can bring up some fear. It is important to stand your ground and know that everything is happening by itself. There is no imaginary thinker of thoughts or doer of deeds. This is simply an idea that has held us captive and now it's time to align with the Being that is not doing anything. Align with it and move into an effortless space where everything you need will come to you.

Over and over again you will be pulled back into the illusion that you are choosing, doing, reaching and trying to get to some perfect place where no suffering occurs. You must remind yourself again and again that *all suffering is in the mind* and that you are the effortless Being that is not on a journey. You are timeless Being itself and time happens inside you. The seeming journey will continue in front of you as you rest as the Beingness.

If resistance continues then re-read the "Self-Inquiry" chapter and the "Short Cut" chapter and apply them. Ask yourself what is aware of this resistance and is IT affected by the resistance?

There is within us all, this essential core that is just Being. It is the potential from which all manifestation arises. Rest as the Beingness and do not allow yourself the vanity of believing yourself to be the cause of thoughts, words and actions. Stop trying to manage your life and know that you are life itself.

CHAPTER 9

Noticing the Sense of Presence

When we begin to really notice what we are we can observe that there is a body present, but there is also something subtle that is here which feels like a "me-ness". Something very subtle is present and we can sometimes notice it in and around the body as a sense of us. It has been described as a sense of a Presence and we can begin to pay more attention to that than the thoughts we have passing through our mind.

Getting in touch with the sense of Presence is easier if we can gently ask the questions "What am I?" and "Where exactly am I?" Allowing these questions to penetrate deeply into our being, we will notice that the answer comes as a Knowingness rather than a thought or verbal answer. We will begin to feel our essence as a kind of subtle energy field or Presence. Something is here and is sentient and awake and when we let go of trying to define what it is exactly and feel for the answer we can find our experience changing. Presence can feel much more expansive and peaceful, open and free, compared with the sense of being someone with a fixed identity and ideas about our own self.

Notice that something is undeniably present in this moment and let go of naming it and immediately you will notice an expansive Presence begins to make itself known to you *AS* you. It has been called many names but it is more subtle than the physical body and easily missed if we are not paying attention.

Noticing the sense of Presence is noticing the sense of "here-ness" and "now-ness" of our Being. "Here" is not the location of the body in a room; it is the sense of being present and aware. "Now" is not a time on the clock that comes before "later" but rather a sense of something being alive and awake right now in this moment. Being present to this Presence will allow you to live in the effortless place and we can discover that our very own sense of Presence is in fact the Presence of God.

The Practice of Feeling the Sense of Presence

Take as much time as you can each day to simply sit down in silence and notice the sense of Presence. The more you pay attention to this sense of Presence the stronger it will seem to get. You need not sit in any particular position but as with each of these practices it is best not to lie down as you may fall asleep.

Simply sit and notice the Presence and any time you notice you are focusing on thoughts, bring the attention back to the Presence. There is no special way to stop the attention from drifting off with thoughts so do not waste time looking for one. As with all the methods described in this book, the success is bringing the attention back to the Noumenon each time it has drifted off. If you sit down for 20 minutes and your attention goes with thoughts 50 times, the successful practise is bring attention back 50 times. Simply do this and you will succeed in dissolving the separate sense of self and all suffering will cease. This IS the way that all awakened beings have reached total Realisation of the Self.

The Progression of the Practice

At first when you begin the practice it may feel like "I am in the Presence"; that there is a "me" that is focusing on the Presence. As you progress, it may begin to feel like the Presence is getting stronger but it is not. All that is happening is that less attention is going to the thoughts and more to the Presence. You must allow yourself to fall in love with this sense of Presence because it is what you are.

Soon it is seen that Presence is simply being present to Itself and there is no "me" other than a thought appearing in this Presence. In the end there is simply the profound Presence and peace.

Summary of the Practice

Simply sit and notice the sense of Presence and each time your attention becomes distracted you must bring it back to the Presence. Do this as many times as is necessary in your practice session.

Resistance to the Practice

You may notice that there is resistance to practicing or to feeling the sense of Presence. When this happens it is usually because our mind is making too much noise to seemingly be able to sense the Presence. It is usual to have some times where we just don't feel like sitting down to pay attention to Presence, but if it continues then it may be that our mind has distracted us or perhaps a particular thought pattern or emotion is coming strongly. Whatever the resistance that comes, it is important to remember that you are stronger than any thought or feeling and to remind yourself why you wish to be free of suffering. *Resistance is suffering* and you simply need to become determined to progress. Most spiritual students fail to see this through but you are different. You chose to pick up a book like this and therefore you will make it.

If resistance continues read the chapter on Self-Inquiry and apply it. Notice that the sense of Presence must be here first for the sense of "me" to appear in; therefore nothing can block your ability to sense this powerful Presence. If you believe a thought which says you're blocked, then you will have a real experience of feeling blocked. Presence is NOT an experience; it is eternal and here and now. It is here before you even ask if it is here.

Also you may find it helpful to read the "Short Cut" chapter and apply what you learn. Continue with your practice as soon as possible.

Presence is the basic sense of existence not polluted by any identity or "me-ness" and as such is worth striving to be able to sense all the time. Nothing can hide this Presence from you because it is you.

CHAPTER 10

Staying in the "I Am"

The only thing we can know for certain is that we are. You know only this with absolute certainty. You know that you are. You know the sense "I Am" and this has been your constant companion with you throughout your life. This feeling that "I Am" is your basic currency, your working capital and you can use it to reach total liberation by focusing on it to the exclusion of everything else.

It is important to clearly understand what the "I Am" is. It is not the thought "I am" which comes AFTER the knowing that "I Am". When you wake up in the morning after a night's sleep you know you are here again and you do not have to think about it. If you regain consciousness after an anaesthetic you do not have to think about whether you exist or not. You know immediately that you ARE and thought will happen after. To even have the thought "I am" then you must BE already to notice the thought.

Staying in the "I Am" is simply the practice of noticing this thoughtless, wordless place called "I Am" and it is as simple as that feeling when you first wake up in the morning. It can also be recognised as that pure stateless state that we knew as infants before we began to think about what we are.

Noticing the sense "I Am" is easy but staying only in that sense may be difficult at first. There will be a tendency to think about the fact that you are. It is easy to bring yourself back to noticing that you are if you want to. Whatever thought has seemed to distract you, simply recognise that you could not have any thoughts pass through your brain if you were not here first to see them.

Gradually you will come to see that "I Am this sense of I Am". You will see that you are life itself. Life IS and You are That.

The Practice of Staying in the "I Am"

Simply sit down each day and take some time to notice this sense of "I Am". Sit for as long as you can and each time you realise your attention has gone back to whatever thoughts are going through your mind, go back to noticing that you are. Thoughts may come and go, emotions may come and go but you must keep your attention on this sense of "I Am" for the duration of the practice session.

It is important to know that nobody can keep attention on the "I Am" all the time. It is natural and part of being human to have our attention wander frequently, but those who will succeed will notice this and bring their attention back to the "I Am" as soon as possible.

You need not sit in any particular position and it's more important that you are comfy and can sit for a few minutes. As you continue to practice each day you may notice that in time you begin to sense the "I Am" at random moments during the day too. It begins to be seen that this pure sense "I Am", which is here before thoughts, is also here when thoughts are present although it may seem to be covered up by the noise of the mind at first. You will come to see that the pure "I Am"

Dissolving The Ego

is always available and peace is ever present if we choose to notice it more than the noise of the mind.

The Progression of the Practice

At first your practice may feel as though you are staying in the "I Am" more and more. It will feel as though you are a separate "me" noticing the "I Am" feeling/sense. As you progress in your practice you will come to see that it is in fact this "I Amness" that is really watching itself. The thought "I am watching the I Am" is appearing in That which is there before any thought.

Gradually we can come to see that all of life is this "I Am" and that there is nothing outside of this. The "I Amness" finally comes to see that "I am this I Am".

Summary of the Practice

Take as much time as you are able to each day to notice this pure wordless and thoughtless place that is here before any thought occurs. It is here at all times and we must put attention on it. As we put attention on it, the idea that we are a separate being, isolated and alone, will gradually begin to dissolve. Be disciplined with regular practice sessions and do not expect any particular results. Simply be concerned with bringing attention back to the "I Am" each time it goes with the phenomena of thoughts, feelings and sensations in the body.

Resistance to the Practice

The biggest resistance to the practice may come because you might have the idea that you cannot find this sense of "I Am" or you do not know what it is. This "I Am" is simply your current awareness or that feeling that "I exist". Stay in that simple sense/feeling as often as you can.

If resistance continues then re-read chapter 21, "Self-Inquiry" and chapter 22, "Short Cut", and apply them. Ask yourself what is aware of this resistance and is IT affected by the resistance?

The sense that "I Am" has to be here before you can have any experience at all. See this clearly and deeply and peace will begin to permeate your life. You must have existence before anything else can happen to you. Simply pay more attention to this sense that "I Am" than anything that comes after it.

CHAPTER II

Tuning Into the Awakeness

Each morning we notice that we are awake and that sense of being awake before any other thoughts come is the focus of this practice. The key with this practice is to notice that sense of Awakeness and exclude all other sensations and thoughts. It is important to know that you can only pay attention to one thing at a time, so if you are noticing the sense of Awakeness then you are automatically excluding everything else. You do not have to make an enormous effort to keep thoughts out of your mind as this is simply not possible; it is enough to pay attention to what you are, which is this Awakeness.

Each morning, something seemingly wakes up from sleep. We just assume that this is "me", which is a sense of being someone; it feels like "I am awake". If we really slow things down and look at what happens when we wake up, we can see that there is this Awakeness present even before our eyes open and before the thought "I am awake now" comes. In truth all we really know for sure is that something is Awake. Some sentience is here and seems to wake up. Some intelligence is here and is aware of its surroundings. If we can disregard thinking about what we are then we will notice that all we really know is that something woke up and this basic sense of

Awakeness is with us throughout the day until we go to sleep at night.

As we focus on this Awakeness only, we will find peace. But if we hold onto the idea that "I am awake" we will be perpetuating this sense of being a separate person. We do not have any proof at all that we are a person or that this person woke up this morning. All we know for sure is that something woke up and we don't know what. It is enough to not know. Stay in this basic sense of Awakeness.

As you move about the day, thoughts will come and go and distract attention to the sense of being "me" that is living my life. It is important to take time each day to notice that the sense of Awakeness that we noticed first is still here. We have to be Awake and Conscious before we can have any thoughts run through our brain. We have to be Awake to even get distracted. Notice how you always have this sense of Awakeness with you during the day — this is in fact why it is called the "waking state". Stay in that simplicity and make no attempt to define what you are.

The Practice of Tuning Into the Awakeness

As we have said before, you can only be aware of one thing at once so it is important to know what to focus on. Most of the day, our focus is automatically going to our sense of identity as a "me" and the thoughts that pass through "my mind". Therefore, we must take some time each day to sit and notice only this sense of Awakeness that is present. It is here all the time but we must choose (was chose) it willingly. To choose it we must only notice it and keep redirecting our attention over and over to it when focus wanders.

Over time it will become apparent that Awakeness is awake but we cannot find any entity called "me" that is awake. By tuning into the pure sense of being Awake we are automatically dissolving the separate sense of self that feels "I am awake". It is that simple. We are either perpetuating the sense of being someone or dissolving it. We dissolve it or perpetuate it with our focus. Attention is really our only faculty and our only choice is what to put the attention on. We can either put it on Truth or falsehood. You must come to a decision point of deep conviction that you want only Truth and maintain your focus on it long enough, consistently, until there is no ability to seemingly lose sight of Truth left in you.

The Progression of the Practice

When you first begin to notice this pure Awakeness, it will seem like it can easily be obscured by thoughts. Thoughts pass by and our attention automatically goes with them, to look at them, out of force of habit. You cannot remove this habit of paying attention to thoughts but you can replace this habit with a new one. You can either pay attention to the thoughtless, wordless Awakeness or to the thoughts that arise in it.

It will feel as though you are making an effort to notice the Awakeness at first, but as you persist in building this habit it will become effortless at some point. *Consistency is the key here.* As it becomes effortless to notice and stay in that simple Awakeness, your true nature will begin to reveal itself to you. You will come to know that all thoughts appear after the Awakeness is awake. Nothing can occur without the Awakeness here first to perceive it. Even the thought "I am awake" must appear in this Awakeness which was already here.

53

Eventually it will be seen that Awakeness is recognising Its own nature and there never was any separate person to be awake or asleep.

Summary of the Practice

The practice is simply to take some time each day, as much as you can, to notice the fact that you are Awake. There is a sentient, intelligent Awakeness present and you simply need to notice this and prefer this state to any other. When you find attention has wandered to the thoughts appearing in the Awakeness, bring attention back to the simplicity of the Awakeness. It is not the thought "I am awake" but rather that state which must exist first before any thought can come.

Do this practice as much as you can each day. At times during the day you may notice the sense of Awakeness spontaneously appearing evident to you. This will happen more and more until eventually you can notice it even when your body is moving and your mind is busy.

At a certain point you will realise you ARE this pure Awakeness noticing Itself and you are not the thoughts that appear in it. Confirm this over and over until you cannot forget it anymore.

Resistance to the Practice

The biggest resistance to the practice may come because you notice there are times when you feel you are unaware of the Awakeness and lost in thoughts. Perhaps at first there may be long periods of time where this seems to be the case. This is normal at first and happens to everyone. The key to breaking through this apparent block is to really understand deeply that you must be here and Awake first, before any block can be noticed. Any block is noticed by you and it can only affect you if you believe yourself to be an object called "me" appearing in the Awakeness. Once you see that Awakeness is constantly present, it becomes obvious that you must be that Awakeness. If you are the silent, invisible, formless, intangible field of Awakeness Itself, then what thought or feeling can possibly block you?

If resistance continues then re-read chapter 21, "Self-Inquiry" and chapter 22, "Short Cut" and apply them. Ask yourself what is aware of this resistance and is IT affected by the resistance?

Awakeness has to be present first, before anything else can be noticed. Without this Awakeness to observe the world, then no world actually exists. Confirm this for yourself and confirm over and over that there is no entity that is awake; but it is in fact Awakeness that is awake.

CHAPTER 12

Be Conscious of Your Consciousness

Everyone has something we all take for granted. We never notice our Consciousness at all until we are under threat of losing it. Consciousness has many qualities but the main one we will focus on here is the power to observe. Consciousness feels like "I" when it observes through a body and when it believes it is the body then it begins to think of itself as a "me". This is how our sense of being separated and isolated came. Most of us let our attention go right to what we are Conscious of such as our thoughts, emotions, relationships and world at large; but as part of this practice we will spend some time each day noticing that we are Conscious.

The key with any of these practices is to ignore the mind's idea that it is simple and easy and quick to do. This must be a continual noticing for periods each day as in meditation. Our mind would like to quickly look and ask "Am I Conscious? Yes I am Conscious. Ok next, now what?" If you allow your mind to dictate this to be a one time noticing then you are robbing yourself of a golden opportunity. Mind likes complexity and would rather think about what you are. You are simplicity itself beginning to notice itself and at first you must make a little effort to not allow your attention to run away. The process of dissolving the separate sense of self is not a "to do" list with option five saying "be Conscious that you are Conscious". You do not notice it and say "Ok done that, check!" It is a process of noticing the obvious and staying in the clarity and simplicity of holding attention on the simple fact you are Conscious.

Each morning this Consciousness seems to appear and we take it to be permanent until each night it disappears and we go to sleep. At some point the Consciousness will go for good as the body expires and you will seem to die along with it unless you maintain steady attention on the Consciousness.

As with each one of these practices, steady attention on the Consciousness will allow it to reveal something amazing to you. It will reveal to you what you are; what is beyond even this waking state that feels like "I am Conscious". If you need some help to find motivation then consider how fragile this Consciousness is. One needle of anaesthetic and you are gone. One injury to the brain and you might be seriously impaired in functioning. One overwhelming experience and you might faint and are gone. I would urge you to find out what does not go. It never came. It is right here now seemingly being obscured by this sense of "I am Conscious". Focus on this sense that "I am Conscious" until it merges and disappears into what has always been here. Stay in the simplicity and each and every time you find yourself drifting along with thoughts bring your attention back. When you have had enough of suffering you will call upon the strength, courage and conviction that is already within you but not yet been activated. You will go beyond any limitation and see how free you have always been.

The Practice of Being
Conscious of Your Consciousness

You can only be Conscious of one thing at a time; attention can only focus on one thing at a time. You will know this for certain if you try to think two thoughts at the same time. Focus your vision on a spot on the wall right in front of you and then try to focus your vision on your feet at the same time and you will see it cannot be done. The great power of Consciousness is its ability to observe. Observing or witnessing thoughts, emotions, people, events and relationships is a kind of focus on them and reinforces the idea that there is a separate "someone" here observing "them" over there. Even when we observe our thoughts it will only serve to reinforce the belief that there is a separate "me" that is here and witnessing these thoughts. Observe your thoughts long enough only to see that you are not them and then turn your Consciousness back upon itself.

Whatever you focus upon you will make disappear. If you observe anything long enough you will see that the name and other descriptive thoughts about it seem to disappear and all that remains is the "Isness" of that thing. You might have noticed that as a child if you ever repeated out loud a word over and over, after a while it loses its familiar meaning and sounds strange to say it at all.

In this practice we are being Conscious only of the fact that we are Conscious. Notice the instruction was not to notice the THOUGHT "I am conscious" but to notice the SENSE of Consciousness that is here before any thought. You have to be Conscious before you can notice the thought "I am conscious". Stay in that noticing of the wordless place before thought.

The fact is that you are Conscious now or else you would not be able to read this. Consciousness comes before anything else is able to be observed. Confirm this fact for yourself. If Consciousness must be present before anything else can be observed doesn't it make more sense to put attention on that Consciousness only, rather than what you are Conscious of? To find out what you are simply pay consistent attention to the Consciousness rather than the objects you are Conscious of, such as thoughts.

The Progression of the Practice

At first as you start the practice it will feel as though you are being Conscious of your Consciousness. It will feel as though you have a choice what to focus on; the sense of Consciousness or the thoughts going through the mind. You must exercise your power of choice and focus consistently on the Consciousness itself until it is automatically chosen; until paying attention to thoughts becomes so uninteresting that you simply disregard whatever the mind tries to sell you.

As you continue the practice you will notice that you are falling in love with Yourself and want more and more to be with Yourself in the truest sense of the phrase. Being Conscious of the Consciousness is the most intimate way to be with yourself. Thoughts are external to you and you will begin to want only this pure Consciousness itself. Soon the idea that you are Conscious will disappear and it is seen that there is only Consciousness that is noticing itself. Eventually even the sense of something subtle noticing itself will go and there will be only This That You Are.

Summary of the Practice

Set aside some time each day to sit down (in any position) and be Conscious of your Consciousness. This is as simple as noticing that there is Consciousness ALREADY present. As soon as your attention becomes hypnotised by thoughts you must bring yourself back to noticing only that you are Conscious.

Consciousness will repeatedly become focused on the thoughts passing through and this is normal. Everyone goes through this stage and nobody found a shortcut to it other than bringing attention back over and over. Repeat this for as long as the practice session continues.

Resistance to the Practice

The majority of people who follow this practice will experience a very similar type of resistance. The thought will soon come that this is boring and attention will wander back to the seemingly more exciting thoughts coming and going. Your role in the process is to keep your focus on the Consciousness long enough that the pull of thoughts begins to lose its power. You are making a higher choice that involves turning away from the receiving the temporary "fix" of identifying with the thoughts and the drama of the sense of "me" and all that is happening to it. As you turn away from this neurochemical transmitter "high" that we get from buying into the thoughts then you will begin to experience a profound sense of peace and that everything is in fact totally ok right now.

Your mind will try to distract you and bring attention back to it by telling you that this practice is getting you nowhere; or that you are not taking responsibility for your life. It will use its tricks to get you to stop the practice and this in itself should tell you that you are on to something. The power of this practice is in its simplicity and your mind knows it is losing ground. Hold your attention on the sense that you are Conscious and watch for the tendency to get distracted.

If resistance continues then read and apply the chapter on Self-Inquiry and on Short cutting the process. It is natural for the mind to resist this practice because it knows that you are near the end of suffering.

Everyone is Conscious and everyone takes this Consciousness for granted. Will you take it for granted? Stay in the simplicity of only knowing that you are Conscious. Be Conscious of your Consciousness.

CHAPTER 13

Noticing the Existence

The fact is that you exist. This is the one undeniable fact in all our lives. We can argue about anything else and we can even argue about what we exist AS but we know for absolutely certain that we have Existence. If we allow ourselves to finally admit that this is the only thing we are certain of then we are getting somewhere. Suffering occurs when we feel as though we know what we are and are sure of it. In the normal human Consciousness we are all convinced that we are individual, separate from each other and from life. We assume this about ourselves and this is reinforced by programming over the years. Once we have accepted this we never question this until we suffer so much in this limiting definition of who we think we are that we are forced to look deeper.

This practice is aimed at getting the focus of attention back onto what we know for certain. As much as our mind may resist this eventually we must come to a moment of honesty where we finally admit that all our thoughts about what we are have not been proven. The only thing we know for certain is that we exist. There is Existence, nobody can deny this. What we exist as is still open to be seen. We cannot find this out by thinking about what we are. Thinking about something is NOT the same as Knowing. Thinking about something is NOT the same as Being it. In much the same way we could think about what it is like to be Chinese, write a book on Chinese culture and to learn to speak Chinese fluently but it is not the same as actually being born and raised in China.

Our mind can only know ABOUT something and not actually Know for certain. Mind is a tool for analysing and thinking about things, coming to conclusions and understandings. To truly know something is to BE it; we can only know what it is like to be Chinese by actually being Chinese. Search within yourself and see that all that has happened up to this point is that you have noticed and listened to thoughts about what you are. It is not your mind's fault that it cannot know what you are; it is not supposed to.

Keep attention on what you know to be true only and what you are will be intuitively revealed to you at the right time. You will know it because you will BE it. You can only think about and know about what you are not.

The Practice of Noticing the Sense of Existence.

The practice is a simple one just like all the others in this book. The key is to simply notice that sense of Existence-something is here and enjoying an Existence. Take some each day to notice what you know to be true which is only that you exist. This is not the same as thinking "I exist" as this is a thought. You must exist before you can notice thoughts arising. Stay in that simple Existence and each time your attention is drawn to thinking about what you are or any other thoughts bring it back to this simple Existence.

Over and over again the mind will try to hook you with thoughts that you are making progress, thoughts about Existence, thoughts that you are getting nowhere and even thoughts about how you are not thinking much anymore! Notice these tricks and stay firmly put in the sense of Existence. It is the thoughtless and wordless place that must be here before any thought can pass through it.

Spend as much time as you can each day in this sense only. Bring attention back over and over and do not look for any results. A wandering mind is just as likely on the first day of practice as the last day before the ego vanishes. The number and frequency of thoughts is no measure of progress. Forget about progress and stay put in your conviction.

The Progression of the Practice

At first you will feel as though there is a separate you that is noticing the sense of Existence. There will be a sense that "I exist as me in this body" and that is ok. You must use this seemingly separate existence to focus only on Existence itself.

As you continue your practice each day you will notice that you begin to feel this sense of Existence at random times, when your mind is quieter or you are doing some task that does not need much mental focus. It will begin to make itself known to you more and more often and you may find that you begin to fall into this quiet peaceful sense of Existence; rather than having to look for it and sit down quietly alone to notice it.

Eventually it will occur to you that you are Existence Itself noticing Itself. You are life itself, not a person who is alive. You are all of Existence showing up right here and now; not a person existing for a time and then perishing. Existence is experiencing Itself through this mind and body but it is not separate from the whole; it IS the whole.

Summary of the Practice

Set aside some time each day to sit down (in any position) and notice that you exist. This is as simple as noticing that there is Existence already here. Make no attempt to figure out, analyse or think about what you exist AS. As soon as you become aware of thoughts and pay attention to them you must bring your attention back to looking only at this sense of Existence.

You can only be aware of this Existence OR the thoughts that are arising in it. You can only notice one thing at a time. It is up to you to bring your attention back each time to Existence and be disciplined. You have spent many "lifetimes" being a separate "me" and watching the end of this Existence seemingly occur. Wouldn't it be better this time to find out directly if you can actually perish with the body? Stay only in this sense of Existence.

There is only Existence noticing itself. The thought "I exist" can only be seen once you exist first to see it.

Resistance to the Practice

As with all of these practices resistance will come in the form of thoughts about the practice and how to do it better. You will be tempted to analyse how you are doing; to focus on pleasant or unpleasant feelings and emotions as they surface. Notice this tendency to get distracted and focus your power by repeatedly bringing yourself back to the simplicity of Existence. You exist before any thought can distract you. Are you even distractible?

If resistance continues then re-read the chapter on "Self-Inquiry" and the chapter on "Short Cut" and apply them. Ask yourself what is aware of this resistance and is IT affected by the resistance?

Existence is all of life and when it flows through a body it feels like "I exist" and we take this for fact. Stay in this sense of Existence and cease using your mind to define what you are. Peace will come upon you and stay if you can resist the complexity of thoughts. Mind is complex; Existence is simplicity itself.

CHAPTER 14

Being the Contextual Field

Consciousness can appear as form or formlessness. We could say that form arises out of formlessness. We know much about the form or content of Consciousness as this is the "thingness" that we know so well. We are taught to focus on the content of our Awareness as a priority and to ignore totally the context. What does this mean in our experience? It means that we do not see our own Self IS the Contextual Field and that what we THINK we are is actually the content of the Field.

When we look for ourselves through Self-Inquiry all we can find is the subtle feeling of "I am here" but we cannot actually find a location to that self. We begin to see that this "I sense" is actually the formless Contextual Field of Seeing. The sense that "I am here" or "I exist" is simply the first content of the Field that we are. Thoughts are the first content that fills our Field. By our very nature, we are more like a Field of space than an object that has a location in time and space. Our body has a location and is affected by time and space but we are not.

We can learn to refocus our attention on the Field itself rather than on the thoughts occurring in it. We can put our Awareness on the space that thoughts are appearing in rather than the thoughts themselves. When we do this we begin to see that nothing could exist without this Contextual Field here first for it to appear in.

No-thing could appear without this Field of no-thingness for it to arise in. Form relies on the formless for its Existence. Without the formless Contextual Field then no thought, emotion, event or relationship could appear in it. Our bodies which are solid objects need this context to appear in and to sustain them; just as the clouds need the sky in which they appear. Content can only appear against the backdrop of context. We know this because we can realise we can only hear the objects of sound against the context of Silence. If we try to listen for a sound in amongst a background of white noise we will not hear it. The Contextual Field is invisible, intangible, ineffable and yet is totally here, now and everywhere. It is omnipresent and never began nor can it have any ending. Beginnings and endings can only occur to the objects appearing in this Contextual Field but not to the Field itself. Through this practice we can begin to see we are the Field Itself and not what is appearing in it. We have taken ourselves to be the "me" which is this subtle content or "thingness" that appears when the body appears. In Truth we are the "no-thing-ness" in which all objects are showing up.

The Practice of Being the Context Rather Than Content

At first you can simply start by noticing that without this formless Field being here already you could not see what thoughts and emotions are appearing in it. Simply said you must be here first before you can observe anything. The Contextual Field is that silent Awareness that is just observing without comment or opinion; it just is.

The practice is to sit down each day for some time in any position that is comfortable and direct your attention to the fact that there is a silent invisible space like Field of Awareness present. As you begin it will feel like "you" but that is all right. We must all start from this feeling that what I am is a kind of diffuse "me-ness". Notice this subtle Field that you are and disregard any content that appears in the Field. You need not try to get rid of thoughts but simply redirect your attention to the Contextual Field itself. In this way the Field begins to focus upon Itself rather than focusing upon the content appearing in it. Time and time again we will be hypnotised into focusing on the thoughts that come rather than on what is aware of all this.

Each time attention goes with thought simply bring it back to that invisible Field that is the context in which all things are arising. Do this as many times as is needed throughout each practice session.

The Progression of the Practice

When you first begin this practice you may have a sense of "I am in the Field" and that is where we must all start from. We think of ourselves as a "something" or "someone" that is appearing in a larger Field. At this stage you might notice the feeling that you are "tuning into" the Field or context of your Existence.

As you progress and become more awake you will see that in fact you ARE this Contextual Field and the sense of you as a person is actually appearing in this infinite You. Eventually you will come to know that all there is IS the Contextual Field and that any seeming content is simply the Field appearing AS something. The Field can appear as nothing or something but it is still the field.

At first it may seem that you have to sit down quietly to notice the Field and ignore all other distractions but as you continue each day you will begin to notice the Field at spontaneous moments. Gradually you will be able to sense the subtlety of the Field itself at any time and no matter what you are doing. In the end you will see that it is the Field noticing itself and that in fact you cannot lose Awareness of the Contextual Field because you ARE the Field.

Summary of the Practice

Take some time each day to notice that silent Contextual Field that is here. Notice this Field and confirm that it must be here first before anything else can appear in it. Each time that your focus gets caught up in thought you must bring it back to the silent Contextual Field. Attention will go with thought over and over as we have been trained to be fascinated by the movement. This is simply a habit that can be replaced by cultivating the habit of focusing on the "nothingness" of the Field.

Each day take as much time as you can to notice and pay attention to the Contextual Field. Confirm again and again that you are the Field Itself and not the content appearing in it. Subtle content like thoughts is still content. Even the "I/me" sense is the content.

Resistance to the Practice

If you experience resistance to practicing that is normal. Our mind has been conditioned since our early development to focus on the content and to totally ignore that which is seeing the content. You are aware enough to know that this does not bring lasting happiness. Identifying with this sense of "me" is really setting yourself up to suffer more.

Develop the conviction that no matter how many times you may get distracted you can always bring attention back. Only one in ten million have awakened fully in the past because they have not had the information, conviction and guidance to do so but now this is changing. The evidence is in your hands and the fact you are reading this means you are ready to finally wake up from this dream. Gather your focus and KNOW that you cannot fail unless you believe you can.

If resistance continues then re-read the chapter on "Self-Inquiry" and the chapter on "Short Cut" and apply them. Ask yourself what is aware of this resistance and is IT affected by the resistance?

As you come to see that what you really are is formless and nowhere to be found in particular you must confirm it over and over again. As you confirm it then the tendency to think of yourself as a "something" or "someone" will disappear and all fear will leave you for good. What can possibly harm you if you know yourself to be the invisible Context in which all is happening? You are the invisible and intangible Contextual Field that is inside, underneath and before the tangible and visible world.

CHAPTER 15

The Ever Present State of Here

This practice is simply one of noticing that no matter where you are in the world, no matter what you are doing or who you are with it always feels like you are Here. There is a simple "Here-ness" about wherever you are. Even if you journey to the end of the universe (if that were possible) it would feel like "I am Here" when you got there. It would never feel like "I am there". "There" is a position in time and space that only has relevance if this sense of "Here" is present.

"Here-ness" is not a geographical location in time and space; it is not a place somewhere on a map. It is a sense of being Present in, around, outside of and before this body was constructed. If you notice when you wake up in the morning you will see the feeling of "I am Here again" is really what is happening. "Here-ness" is an intelligent Field of energy that is perceivable as a constant in your life. Look back at any experience you had previously and confirm that it always happened "Here" and that it always felt like "I am experiencing this Here and Now". It is not possible to get away from this "Here-ness"; even if we say "oh I was daydreaming and I was somewhere else for a minute" it was still happening Here and now.

This "Here-ness" is a subtle Presence that is noticeable but not by our normal senses. If you have ever noticed a feeling that something or someone is behind you and turned around to look but found nothing; notice with hindsight that the feeling was as if something or someone was approaching the proximity of your "Here-ness". Some Presence touched your subtle Field of "Here-ness" and you noticed this. How would this be possible if you are only this physical body?

This sense of "I am Here" is the feeling of being "someone" that is located in this physical body and that is how the practice must begin. As you continue in your practice you will notice more and more simply the sense of being Here comes upon you and it is not a thought "I am Here". You begin to notice simply that "Here-ness" is constant and "I am Here" comes and goes because it is a thought appearing in the "Here-ness" itself.

"Here-ness" is not just where you are; every sentient being is having this same feeling of "Here-ness". Consider for a moment if it were possible for you to inhabit another body than yours. If somehow your Consciousness could be put in another person's body it would still feel to you in this other body as if you were "Here". You would look back at your original body and it would be "over there" and not Here.

You can only think a thought "Here" and you cannot think a thought "over there".

You can only smell a smell "Here" and you cannot smell it over there. It is registering in consciousness "Here". You cannot feel any emotion or have any experience "over there". It has to be felt or experienced "Here" and "Now".

Helen Hamilton

The Practice of Noticing the
Ever Present "Here-ness"

The practice is very simple here as always; take some time each day to sit down and be alone. Put your attention on this sense of "Here-ness" and keep it there. Do not try hard to hold attention on the "Here-ness" but simply notice when attention has gone with thoughts and bring it back to the simple sense of "Here-ness". At first it may feel as if "I am Here" is what is being noticed and that is ok.

The practice is to take attention away from what is happening in the "Here-ness" (such as thoughts about what is here, why you are here etc, emotions, events, noises in the environment or sensations in the body) and put it only on the "Here-ness" itself. Over and over again during the practice session you will find attention has wandered again. There is no need to analyse why you get distracted-this is simply your mind's way of distracting you even more. Stay focused on the sense of being Here and turn away from all other sensations and thoughts.

The Progression of the Practice

As you begin the practice you may notice the thought appearing that "I am Here" and this is ok, as soon as you are able to put attention on the "background" of "Here-ness" in which this thought (and every thought is appearing). It is a shift of focus from thoughts to that which thoughts arise out of. Thoughts can only appear in this "Here-ness" and so as you continue your practice it will seem as though more and more you are able to notice the "Here-ness" directly. Thoughts will seem to become less and less relevant.

74

You will notice certain thoughts coming up that seem to magnetically pull your focus away from the Noumenon and you are noticing the thoughts that are appearing in the "Here-ness". Remind yourself that you can only focus on one thing at once and confirm your conviction to wake up fully. It is just a thought that says "certain thoughts are harder to turn away from than others". Thoughts are all the same; the only difference is what meaning, relevance and belief power we give them.

As you progress further the sense that "I am Here as a separate person" will begin to recede and the "Here-ness" that is unchanged by any experience will show itself to you at random moments unasked and unsearched for. In the end it will be seen that you are this "Here-ness" and the feeling that "I am Here" was just a repeated thought that came with having a physical body for a short time. "Here-ness" is noticing It's own inherent omnipresent nature.

Summary of the Practice

Set aside some time each day to sit down (in any position) and notice this sense of "Here-ness". If you have any difficulties tuning into this start with the thought "I am Here" and then go beyond the thought to see that this thought can only appear when you are "Here". "Here-ness" is noticeable because it must be here before any thought shows up and is recognised.

Each time you notice attention has gone with thoughts, emotions or sensations in the body simply bring it back to the "Here-ness" feeling. Do this as often as is needed each practice session and pay no attention to any thoughts about your progress and how it is going. These are all irrelevant distractions that are tricks of the mind.

Notice the "Here-ness" in moments when you are not formally meditating when you can too. It is easier to do this when the mind is not too busy and when doing tasks that seem mundane and perhaps boring. Tune in as often as you can and It will begin to tune in to you!

Resistance to the Practice

It is very normal to notice a lot of resistance to practising especially at first; as you persist you will find that the resistance falls away. It only comes because you think that it can stop you. This is just a thought. You are that "Here-ness" in which the thoughts about resistance and the resistance itself is appearing. Recognise this and you will come to see that nothing and no thought can stop you. Confirm this. Even resistance, a feeling of restlessness or other distractions can be used as part of your practice. Resistance can only happen "Here". A feeling of restlessness can only occur "Here" and not "over there". Use whatever your mind serves up to you as fodder to help you realise your true nature.

If resistance continues then re-read the chapter on "Self-Inquiry" and the chapter on "Short Cut" and apply them. Ask yourself what is aware of this resistance and is IT affected by the resistance?

When is it not Now? And when are you not Here? You can only arrive somewhere else "Now" and when you get there it will feel like "Here". You cannot reach your destination earlier or later; only Now. You cannot arrive at the "somewhere else" place because when you do it will feel like "Here"

You are this "Here-ness" and "Now-ness". They are your constant companions throughout your entire life and are your Immortal Self. These are the keys to end all suffering.

CHAPTER 16

The Stateless State of Now

Throughout your entire life and even in this moment there has been one thing that has been constant and that is the "Now-ness" of this moment. There is something unique and alive about this moment that is happening that is not present when we think of the past or the future. When we remember the past all that is really happening is neurons are firing in our brains to recall Now. When we worry about or imagine the future we are actually doing it in this moment Now.

Reality is this Now and it is beyond time and space. If you look back at any moment you have experienced you will notice that it was stamped with this feeling of Now. The "stateless state" that is Now and Always is ever present and it is this Now-ness that gives everything you experience its feeling of being "Real". If this Now-ness is ever-present then it must in fact be what we are. Every time we have a sense of a personal "me" that is moving through a separate existence for a set duration we can only notice it Now. When this sense of "me" first came with the body this Now-ness watched it appear. When it is time for the body to end and the "me" to end, this Now-ness will watch it disappear too. The Now is present right now. Contemplate for a moment if you can read this book any other time than Now? Can you do any action, speak any words, think any thoughts any other time than Now? Whatever is happening to you is always happening Now. No other time really exists in Reality.

Now-ness is not the relative "now" of clock time; it is not earlier, now or later we are speaking about here. It is the one constant moment that is eternal. Everything is present here in this moment. There is nothing you can do to be outside of this Now and nothing you need do to return to this Now. Every time you try to do something it will happen in this Now-ness. Recognising this we can begin to see that what we are "feels" like Now-ness; a kind of ongoing moment that lasts forever. Our mind would like us to believe that each experience is happening in a segment of time and that our life is made up of many moments that can be described as now, another now, another now, yet another now and so on. When we really begin to question this we see that it is all one continual Now that has been ever-present. Look back at your life and see if any experience you have had happened "later" or "earlier". These terms of later and earlier do not exist in Reality; they are only mental constructs or concepts. Time and space only appear once we feel ourselves to be a separate entity that is bound by time and space. When we feel separate and that we are located in one place and time then distance, movement and duration of time to travel from one place to another arises.

Time and space only appear once the separate sense of "me" appears. Confirm this for yourself. Even if you make an effort to "stay in this Now" moment you will begin to see that even if you feel you failed to stay in the Now, you failed Now. You cannot be anywhere other than here and Now.

When we see that this Eternal Now-ness is what we are then we can keep our attention on it and allow it to rid us of all our suffering. Suffering and struggle only occurs when time arises. As a separate "me" we spend all our life trying to get a better moment than we had in the past. We regret the past and fear the future.

When you are this Now-ness then time stops and all suffering ceases.

The Practice of Noticing the Now-ness

Noticing the Now-ness is simply exactly as it sounds. We can simply set aside some time each day to notice that whenever we look for it this Now-ness is ever present. Simply keeping attention on this "empty" state of Now and removing attention from thoughts, feelings, events and the world in general is enough. You are already this Now-ness and so you simply need to stop imagining yourself to be "someone" living in this Now-ness. It is enough to take some time each day to sit and notice the Now-ness. Each time your attention goes back to the "me" sense and what you are thinking, feeling or experiencing you must bring attention back to this Now-ness. As you hold attention on this Stateless State of Now you will begin to feel a sense that you are indeed much more than you had believed yourself to be. Consistently paying attention to what you already are, this Now-ness, is enough to begin to break the illusion of thinking that you are a "someone" moving around in time and space that is trying to find peace, love and joy.

The Progression of the Practice

As you begin your practice it will feel as though you are a separate person who is experiencing this Now moment. There will be a sense that "I am experiencing Now" or "I can sense this Now-ness". This is the way we must all start and it is good. As you continue to practice you will notice that gradually this feeling of being someone who is putting attention on the

Now-ness will begin to recede and you will feel more and more that there is just this Now-ness. It will become as though Now-ness is recognising itself or you could say that it will be seen that the Now-ness is eternally here and this feeling of being someone separate from it is seen to be untrue.

The ultimate realisation is that Now-ness is all there is and everything is this Now-ness. This idea of "me" that was so strongly believed in is seen to be just a thought that comes and goes as necessary.

Summary of the Practice

Take some time each day to notice this Now-ness that is always here. Each time attention moves to thoughts, emotions, sensations in the body or any noises in the environment simply bring it back to the Now-ness in which all this is occurring. Repeat this as many times as is needed throughout each practice session. Remain resolute in your resolve and wish to be totally free.

Resistance to the Practice

Resistance to this practice may come in all the other ways described in the other chapters but also it may come because you feel you cannot sense this Now-ness clearly enough to focus on it. This is very common and normal and the way to get around this is to remember you are tuning into the Noumenon which is never going to feel like a thought, "aha" moment, emotion or sensation. We are learning to perceive that which cannot be felt through the senses; it is not a coming and going, a smell, thought, feeling or noise. We are learning to notice that which is always Here and is more of a background Awareness at first. Stop trying to look for a "something" and notice the "no-thingness" is always there. This Now-ness does not feel like anything. It does not taste like anything and it is not an experience which will come and go. It is that in which all experience is occurring; the background or formless substrate for your experiences to happen in.

If resistance continues then re-read the chapter on "Self-Inquiry" and the chapter on "Short Cut" and apply them. Ask yourself what is aware of this resistance and is IT affected by the resistance?

Now is all there is. Everything that emerges out of Now is made of this Now-ness. There are no problems or suffering possible in this Now. There is no future to fear and there is no past to regret. When the future gets here it is always Now. When the past happened it was always happening Now.

CHAPTER 17

Recognising the Knower

Before you even think about something you must know that you exist to be able to have any thoughts. This Knowing is the key to finding out who you are and to dissolving the separate sense of self. If you look back at your life you will see that whatever happened to you there was something that just knew what was happening. If you burn your arm on a hot surface you KNOW it is hot, you don't have to think about it. If you are feeling fear you KNOW that it is fear, you don't have to think about it. If you have a very noisy mind you KNOW it is noisy, you don't have to think about it.

Looking at all of our thoughts, emotions, sensory experiences and life in general we can see that this Knowing has been there all the time. Something in us Knows when we wake up in a morning and it Knows when it is time for sleep in the evening. It Knows but it does not comment on anything. It Knows and silently registers everything.

We can only Know something if it is separate to us or outside of us. We can only see something if it is NOT us. Just as your eyes can see everything but they cannot see themselves, so too you are the Knowing of everything. You are That which Knows. You Know when thoughts come, you Know this sense of existence, you Know when the mind is quiet or noisy, you Know when the body hurts or feels good, you Know what is happening in your environment, you Know many things and yet they must be external to you in order for you to Know about them.

Consider for a moment that you can Know your body is here but your body cannot Know you are here. It is a one-way process. Our thoughts, emotions, perceptions, opinions and world are all things we Know but they cannot Know us because they are not sentient. Thoughts cannot think themselves or know themselves. They are not self-aware. Thoughts need this Knowing to be seen and You are that Knowing. Emotions cannot feel themselves because they are not self-aware. Contemplate these words deeply. Do you not Know even this sense of existence? This existence is Known to you but you are not that which exists in time and space. You Know this sense that "I exist" or "I am" and therefore this is not you. You even Know time and space and therefore even these are "external" to you! Ponder deeply the gravity of what you just read.

If we look in the dictionary for a definition of "to know" we find that it means "to be aware of through observation" or "to have developed a relationship with". Both of these definitions point to the fact that in us all is Something that Knows everything else but is in fact before and beyond everything it Knows. This Knowing Knows even the universe itself. You are this Knower and this practice is simply to keep attention on the Knowing. What usually happens is that our attention is always on WHAT we Know and not the Knowing itself. Here we are shifting the focus back to the fact that there is always this ever-present Knowing here. Keeping attention on the Knowing will dissolve the separate ego or the sense that all you are is the mind and body. This is the end of all suffering.

Helen Hamilton

The Practice of Recognising the Knower

Take some time each day to sit alone and without external distractions; as much time as you are able to. Put attention on that which Knows within you. There is a sense of some Presence within you that just Knows and is not thinking. Thinking happens after this Knowingness is here. You are that which Knows the mind is thinking. Keep your attention here and each time it wanders to thoughts bring it back to the Knowing itself.

As you continue to practice you may find that feelings of peace, bliss, intense energy and more begin to come and you must keep your focus on the Knower of even these feelings. There is no need to push bliss away but simply to notice the Knower instead. You will not lose the bliss, peace or intense Stillness by taking attention off it; in fact the opposite is true. When you keep your focus on YourSelf (the Knower) then peace and love and bliss will be yours always.

The Progression of the Practice

As you begin the practice it will feel as though you are the one Knowing. There will be a feeling of "I Know". This is normal and this is where everyone must start from. This sense of being someone that Knows whatever thoughts, feelings, sensations and events that are happening in your world will stay with you for a while as you continue your practice.

If you are consistent in your practice and want nothing other than to fully awaken and dissolve your egoic sense of self you will soon begin to notice that the sense of Knowing seems to have no source. When we look for the Knower we cannot find it. It is not locatable somewhere as a "thing". Soon it will become very obvious that there is Knowing but no entity that

84

Knows. The source of this Knowing cannot be found. If you look for it somewhere you will not find it. Instead it will be seen that you are this Knowing and not a person that knows.

Gradually you will find that the Knowingness begins to present Itself to you at random moments more and more often. Less and less will you have to look for it and at some point you will notice it seems to be always here. In fact it is that your attention is simply no longer wandering away with thoughts. Gradually the practice sessions will begin to happen more often and spontaneously you will recognise this ever present Knowingness is what you are.

In the end it will be seen that this Knowingness is what you are and all that you Know is arising out of this Knowingness. There never was any separate person that Knows; it just appeared that way for a while.

Summary of the Practice

Take some time each day to sit alone and without distraction and notice the Knower. Notice the fact that this Knower is there before even thought occurs. Each time you become distracted by your attention wandering off with thoughts simply bring it back to the Knower. Repeat this for as many times as is necessary throughout the practice session. Turn away from all distractions of noise, sensations, feelings and thoughts and keep attention only on the Knower.

Resistance to the Practice

This practice is extremely direct and as such it may invoke resistance from your mind. The mind will not want to keep attention in one place only as it is used to jumping from subject to subject again and again. As you begin the practice you may notice some level of resistance, excuses, reasons why it will not work and all other kinds of thoughts coming up to distract you. This should show you that you are onto something good!

The amount of resistance to doing this is directly proportional to the effectiveness of the practice. Of course your ego will not want you to do this practice as it knows it is on a timer or countdown to disappearing. You must be strong and have a firm conviction that you will not be dissuaded. Nothing is stronger than the absolute conviction to wake up fully in this lifetime for it invites a whole plethora of unseen help from Divinity and you will be greatly assisted.

If resistance continues then re-read the chapter on "Self-Inquiry" and the chapter on "Short Cut" and apply them. Ask yourself what is aware of this resistance and is IT affected by the resistance?

When the Knower turns attention upon Itself it will come to Know Itself as the Infinite Knowingness/Awareness/ Presence that always IS and always will be. There is no separate "me" that knows; all we can find is that Knowingness is occurring seemingly with no locatable source in time and space.

CHAPTER 18

Recognising Your Own Subjectivity

We have been conditioned or trained to perceive ourselves to be an object; what we have been used to defining ourselves as is this subtle sense of being a "someone" in or with a body. This sense of being someone is really just a collection of thoughts about "me" and what I like or don't like, my dreams, hopes and goals, failures, my past regrets and future wishes and more. This all coagulates together to become our sense of self and is really a subtle object.

An object is a thing that has a definable location and duration in time and space. We are used to calling solid things objects such as a table, a planet, a human body or an apple. As humans we tend to disregard the subtle objectivity of thoughts, emotions and sensations in the body; all this we put together and call it "me". I want you to begin to examine if "me" is Subjective or objective. Was this sense of "me" here before the body was? Will it still remain after the body goes? Anything that relies on the body for its Existence, such as thought which needs a brain to think it, must be finite or in actuality an object. The sense of "me" is perhaps the most subtle object of all as it is always coming and going; it is not there when we have no body and it is not there in deep sleep, coma or when under an anaesthetic.

What is this all driving at? It is to get you to realise that thoughts, feelings and emotions come and go and therefore MUST be objects having a finite life span in time and space. So too must your body be an object as it will go just as it came one day.

All that you can perceive are objects-stop for a moment and confirm this to be true before continuing. Can anything that you perceive be other than an object?

Now turn attention to what is perceiving; is that an object? If you the Perceiver of all thoughts, emotions, bodies, time and space were an object then you must have a location — when we look for this location we find only "no-thingness". The sense of "me" can be seen to be a subtle object yet the One seeing this cannot be seen. We begin to realise that what we really are is the Subjective "nothingness" that is watching all objective "thingness". You can stop right now and see if you can find the one that Knows/Sees/Perceives the "me" or person feeling. You will not be able to find it anywhere in a place. It is the Placeless Place.

The first time you realise that what you are is this pure Subjectivity it can be quite shocking but it will become more obvious as you confirm it again and again. The aim of this practice is to reverse the tendency to think of yourself as an object. Objects like thoughts will be there but they are always appearing in (and witnessed by) this Subjective Self. Keeping attention on the Subjectivity and not allowing it to go back to the passing phenomena of objects allows the Truth of what you are to be revealed to you.

The Practice of Recognising
Your Own Subjectivity

This practice is as simple as sitting down each day quietly for a period of time and putting your attention on the Subjective sense of a Witness that is watching thoughts. Notice that you cannot find it in any particular place and yet something is here and observing. Notice that it must be this Subjective sense of Self that can see objects. Objects cannot observe themselves. A thought cannot notice itself, nor can an emotion witness its own coming and going. No matter what object comes and goes you are there to witness it as this Subjective observer.

When attention drifts onto watching objects such as thought, feelings, opinions and narratives of the mind simply redirect the attention to that Subjectivity. Keeping attention consistently each day on this pure Subjectivity will cause the sense of being an object or a "someone" to dissolve. Thinking of yourself as an object or a definable "me" that is in the body is the cause of all fear. When we believe ourselves to be a finite entity bound by time and space we will also always fear the ending of this imaginary entity one day.

See clearly that you are not a "something" or a "someone" but you are the pure sense of Subjective witnessing Itself; but there is no person witnessing. See this and be free as no ending can come for This That Is because it never began.

The Progression of the Practice

When you first begin to take time each day to sit down and notice this Subjectivity you might encounter the tendency to think of yourself as an object. Remember that an object need not be solid like a table — but it can be anything that has a start and an ending.

It will feel at first as though you are a separate person noticing this "bigger" and more expansive sense of Subjective Self that is witnessing everything. As time passes and you continue to practice daily you might find that you begin to think of yourself as this Nothingness that is purely a Subjective experience. This pure Subjectivity will begin to reveal itself to you at random moments during the day when you are not trying to put attention on it or formally practicing. Gradually the idea that you are making a decision to sit down and notice this Subjectivity will disappear into the knowingness that this Subjective sense of Self is beginning to notice Itself more spontaneously.

Eventually any sense of being separate from this pure Subjectivity will disappear and you will know you have always been this and all there is, is This. There is nothing else.

Summary of the Practice

Take some time each day to sit by yourself and free from distractions. Sit for as much time as you can manage and keep attention only on the Subjective nature of the Witness or Perceiver. That which watches all thoughts is purely Subjective, a no-thing-ness, and it must begin to watch Itself. In watching, it sees it cannot find Itself in any particular location and yet it seems to be present in every particular location!

When attention drifts to thoughts, emotions, noises in the environment or sensations in the body simply bring it back to the pure Subjective Witness watching Itself.

Resistance to the Practice

Time and time again you will find you keep thinking of yourself as an object. This is simply a habit that has been reinforced over and over again. We have been trained or conditioned to only notice the objective nature of ourselves and to totally ignore the Subjective. For this reason you may find it frustrating at first when you observe the amount of times this habit comes into play but you must persist. Every awakened Being has gone through this process and persisted until the habit disappeared. We cannot simply force a habit to stop but we CAN replace it with another habit. All of these practices are simply to give your attention something healthy to focus on. When attention begins to focus on what is your Truest Self then all that is false will begin to dissolve and it gathers speed. The effects are cumulative and one day quite by surprise you will find yourself freer than you ever thought possible.

If resistance continues then re-read the chapter on "Self-Inquiry" and the chapter on "Short Cut" and apply them. Ask yourself what is aware of this resistance and is IT affected by the resistance?

You already are this pure Subjectivity and there is no need to try to get rid of the objects you perceive. You need only keep attention on the Subjectivity itself; rather than the usual habit of being fixated and fascinated on the thought objects passing by you. Subjectivity is what is here. No entity can be found that is watching. Reality is this pure Subjectivity — it does not need any objects at all.

CHAPTER 19

Stage Two Practice: Trigger Events

Once we have established a good practice routine, we will begin to find it easier and easier to tune into the Silence, Stillness, Awareness or the Noumenon by whichever name we call it. This is the stage when we may begin to feel like we are being tested. Events in our lives can trigger positive or negative thoughts and emotions based on whether they fit with our projections and desires.

Although it may feel as though we are being tested it is not by some higher power or all-seeing entity that is determined to stop our progress or define our worthiness for awakening. The test comes when an event happens in our world that triggers a lot of thoughts and emotions (and the resulting tensions in the body) to be felt. This is a crucial stage in our practice and one that we must understand if we are to wake up fully. We are being shown in these moments where we are still believing ourselves to be separate entities or where we are listening to our egoic sense of self.

When thoughts are triggered, we have two options and we will look at each in turn. We can (and usually do) pay attention to them and experience emotions based on how much those thoughts are believed. Thoughts are phenomena and they emphasise the feeling of being a "someone" that is thinking and feeling the resulting emotions. When we believe these thoughts, we are automatically reinforcing our sense of being separate.

The other option is to allow the thoughts to come and the emotions too and yet remain focused on the Noumenon Itself by whatever means you tune into it. At first this may seem very difficult but it is only because the force of habit is to take attention away from the Noumenon and give it to the thoughts. A habit may be well established in our Consciousness but it is still just a habit which can be undone by paying attention to the Noumenon.

The only choice we have is whether to pay attention to the thoughts in moments like these or to turn away from the magnetic pull of the thoughts and stay with the Noumenon. Allow the body and mind to feel whatever they are feeling and remain centred on the Silence, Stillness or sense of Existence. Immediately you will begin to feel peace again and the emotional charge will begin to dissipate. If we remain focused on the pure Awareness we will find it easier and easier each time. The urge to pay attention to thoughts is simply a habit of where to put your attention; as you have seen when you are meditating and so can be reversed. The question is — will you?

A Thousand Small Moments

We begin to live our awakening fully by being willing to turn away each time something triggers within us this strong sense of being someone that something has just happened to. No matter what thoughts come up from a trigger event it IS possible to simply take attention away from the thoughts and to say an inward "thank you" for being shown where you are still paying attention to thoughts.

Remember we can only pay attention to one thing at once; our attention is either on thoughts and phenomena or on the Silence. We are either strengthening our sense of being separate and our ability to suffer or we are dissolving the separateness. We cannot do both; the choice is always ours and we must make it every time.

In one thousand tiny moments such as these a Sage is made. Each one of us has this inner power, focus and conviction to turn away from the magnetic pull of thoughts and focus back on our True Self. It is a choice between peace and suffering. Choice by choice we bring our lives back into harmony moment by moment. This is the path of those who have awakened and there is no big secret to learn other than the fact that you can ignore any thoughts no matter how alluring they may seem to be.

When you become resolute in your decision to stay in the Noumenon AS the Noumenon then all unseen powers come to help you.

Stage One Practice Prepares You For This

By now you should have at least tasted the true Silence that you are. By spending time on one of the stage one practices you have prepared yourself for stage two. Knowing that you are this peace, love and freedom and having felt it even for a short while, or in ever increasing frequency in your life will show you that it is worth putting the effort in for as long as it takes to turn away from thoughts when you are tested. Only by learning how to quickly and easily tune in to the Silence or Pure Beingness can you hope to do so when your mind is telling you many reasons why you cannot.

It takes great strength of character to turn away from thoughts that are telling you how unfair this situation is, how you are right and the other person is wrong, how this should not be happening and how much it hurts you. Thoughts will insist on telling a story around each event that triggers the separateness of the egoic self within you but you need not listen to the stories. You are not the one telling stories NOR are you the one affected by the stories. You are the Beingness itself from which the idea of being someone is appearing.

Use Everything You Are Given

Every event that happens and triggers suffering within you is really a great gift. It is life's way of showing you what you have not been willing to see until now. It may seem greatly unfair that the moment you are determined to stay as the Silence that all kinds of mental noise begins to make itself known to you. It may seem that when you are triggered into a thought pattern and resulting emotional state of discord that you are further away than ever from your goal. This is not the case. Life is simply showing you where you are still buying into the idea of separation; of being a "somebody" that has rights, feelings, needs, desires and goals. Life is giving you an opportunity to look at what thoughts are routinely believed in these moments and to turn back to Silence.

Anyone can adore the Silence when our mind is quiet or when we are sitting alone in our meditation space. When the mind is NOT quiet then we will find out how much we love Silence or if we trade Silence for the temporary buzz of feeling unjustly treated, outraged, upset, angry, triggered, saddened, jealous or any other state. All these states require you to believe the idea you are a separate entity.

If you are really serious about waking up fully then use everything you are given. Don't just order one thing from the menu of life — order everything. Ask for whatever it takes for you to wake up and mean it. Ask to be shown every place in your life where you are buying into noise and avoiding Silence. Be willing to see that which you have not wanted to see before. You see it is not so important to look at each thought pattern, emotion or sensation that comes up when you are triggered into some old reaction; but more important to look at your attention and to see whether it goes to the thoughts in a knee jerk response or if it stays with the Silence. If your attention stays in Silence it will very quickly not matter at all to you whether your mind is quiet or having a tsunami.

Use everything that happens in your life as a tool to help you wake up. Begin to look for reactions mentally, emotionally and physically. Take stock of your life and see which people, events, places or situations routinely trigger a mental and emotional response that seems to have a life of its own. These reactions have grown strong because of our habit of giving them attention. Attention feeds whatever you focus it upon with energy. You get more of what you pay attention to very quickly. Remember that attention can either be on the Silent Noumenon or on the noisy phenomena of thoughts and emotions, not both.

Win Yourself Back

When these moments come up for you it becomes obvious that the common factor is some kind of identification with being a person, separate from everything else. All that is needed is to disengage from feeding thoughts and emotions with your attention. Although it may seem difficult at first to keep your attention on the Stillness when thoughts come up, each time you hold the intention to stay in the Stillness it makes it easier.

Each one of the thousand moments is like a chance to win a part of yourself back and with each victory you will grow in strength, conviction and confidence in the process. You will begin to see that the ability to suffer is there only because it has not been investigated and the idea of being someone alone and separate has been allowed to persist simply through a lack of clear seeing.

When something happens in your life that causes upset, suffering and identification with being a separate person know that it is not because you are not good enough at the practice. On the contrary, it is because of your conviction and pure intention to win back your freedom that these things are happening. Here life is showing you "Win yourself back here... and here....and here too". Life is helping you, your mind is helping you by showing you where you still are more interested in thoughts than in YourSelf.

If you can begin to develop an attitude of being grateful for these trigger moments you will find yourself beyond the reach of suffering once and for all very quickly. Knowing you do not need to concern yourself with what to do about the outer situation and working on the inner situation first is key. Of course if action needs to happen in the outer world that is fine, take the action you need to but always do the inner work too. Most times the outer situation will begin to resolve just as a result of not buying into and energising the thoughts.

As you continue to stay in the Stillness even when these thoughts come to you then you will begin to become aware of patterns of the mind that you could not see before. You will gather your strength and power back each time you win some of yourself back from the mind patterns. More patterns will become easier to see and you will notice an ability slowly but surely to not automatically go with the thoughts. Each time you overcome you get stronger and the next one becomes easier and easier. Eventually you will find that simply seeing a mind pattern is enough to dissolve it and that staying as the Stillness is effortless even when your mind is making a lot of noise.

This whole process is much quicker, easier and simpler than your mind would have you believe! These thoughts are the reason most people do not make it to full awakening. Will you listen to them?

CHAPTER 20

Stage Three Practice: Constant Effortless Meditation

As you become more established in your daily practice of formal meditation you will begin to notice that informal meditation is happening more often also. What this means is that you will begin to notice more and more often that the Noumenon is just very obviously here and you will not have to search for it.

As your practice deepens you will find that there will be times when your mind is engaged with doing something simple such as driving, cooking or listening to music and all of a sudden you will hear the Intense Silence that you are. Perhaps whilst sitting down after a day's work you will suddenly notice the Immovable Stillness. In these ways and a thousand more that I cannot possibly write down you will find the beauty, love, peace, Stillness, Silence and Awareness just presenting itself to you over and over again. Things that were once unlovable will suddenly move you to tears. Listening to music will become a whole body experience. The sunset may captivate your attention and cause you to be moved with emotion at the wonder of it.

When you begin to notice the Noumenon spontaneously you will find that more and more you want to tune in. Against the background of normal activities we must all do, such as picking up the kids from school or going to work, we will begin to fall in love with the Noumenon.

Fall in Love With YourSelf

Notice that your body prefers to focus on the Noumenon rather than phenomena. Notice how relaxed and calm the body is when you are tuning in. Even your mind will want to turn towards this loving embrace of "sinking into" the Noumenon more and more. Gradually you will find that more often meditation is just happening by itself and that there is nobody making the decision to tune in. More and more the only thing you want to do is to sit and feel the Noumenon. Allow this to occur.

Your mind will tell you that you will lose the ability to function in the world if you let go fully into this desire to sink deeper into the Self. This is simply not true. Over time you will see that it is possible to work, drive, eat, walk, shop and do anything whilst tuning in. Activities always have been happening by themselves and you can simply watch the body do whatever it needs to do. Let go of being the manager and be the witness only. Watch your life from the viewpoint of the Noumenon and you will begin to see that all activities happen effortlessly and do not need your input to continue. Just as you are not remembering to breathe or make your heart beat then you are not remembering to think or do.

You will notice that there are times when the Noumenon seems to be stronger or the Silence seems louder but this is simply because thoughts are quieter or you have all your attention on the Silence. When the "I am doing" thought begins to be no longer believed by you then the Silence will be with you always.

Here are some ways the mind/separate sense of self claims it is necessary for your survival and should not be abandoned. It will tell you that:

"I am driving", "I am thinking", "I am planning", "I am sleeping", "I am enlightening", "I am exhausted".

None of this is occurring in Reality; all these are what the body is doing, not You. You do not sleep, eat or drive. You simply ARE.

Begin to question the reality of these thoughts and beliefs and you will see that all is occurring by itself and the sense of "me" claiming authorship is happening a split second after the action happens or the thought appears. You are only the Witness.

There is no doer of activities and no thinker of thoughts.

Eventually you will rest all the time in the effortless Silence and see that there never was any separate entity that is responsible for running your life. You will find that quite naturally what needs to get done happens by itself and this has always been the case. The separate sense of self has simply been claiming credit for actions, thoughts and feelings that occur spontaneously, arising out of the Noumenon.

This mysterious sense of "me" has claimed that all actions, ideas and beliefs are due to it and it alone. Then it prides itself on the seeming successes and berates itself over the failures. None of this is happening in Reality. All is happening by itself; orchestrated by the whole universe.

You Are Home

If you really want to wake up and you nurture the falling in love with the Noumenon then at some point you will be deeply rewarded by clear seeing. You must hold your ground and stand firm until constant meditation is effortless and is going on by itself. When this occurs you will suddenly know that you are witnessing even the Silence and Stillness. It will become obvious suddenly that you are Watching from Nowhere and that even Beingness is seen from this placeless place. This is the Absolute Reality. You are here before even Stillness or Silence. Presence presents Itself to You.

It will be seen that there is no "me" appearing in the Silence and that in fact You are That which Silence is heard in.

Enough said about this — find out for yourself as an experience and not as words on a page. BE this. It is worth any effort to be free finally and forever.

CHAPTER 21

Self-Inquiry

There are times during our stage One and Two practice where we will come up against what seem to be very difficult obstacles which we cannot overcome. What are these obstacles? Belief in being a person that is attached to a person, place, thing or event and that we need this person, thing, place or event to make us happy. Quite often these attachments can have so much emotional charge around them that it can seemingly eclipse our ability to sense the Noumenon for a while.

An example may be that we are sitting in formal practice and we feel deep peace and then suddenly we begin to experience fear about losing our sense of being someone. No matter what we do we lose the focus and our attention seems to go directly to the thoughts and emotions which seem to have the pull of enormous gravity. Or we may be in Stage Two and out walking and some event triggers anger within us for example and it becomes so intense that we are shaking and perspiring and cannot seem to notice the Noumenon even if we remember what we are supposed to be doing.

These are examples of where Self-Inquiry can help us and it is a very useful technique which helps to dissolve emotional, mental and energetic charge around a thought or belief. Some beliefs have been so ingrained and repeated throughout many lifetimes that we may need an extra tool in these moments.

What is Self-Inquiry?

All of our suffering comes because we assume that we know what we are. If we really look at all of our beliefs about ourselves we come to see they are all based upon the fact we believe that we are this mind and body; that this sense of "I" is only this. We assume this and simply never question it again. Because this belief is so deeply believed it has a lot of energy and belief from us around it. The habit and tendency to automatically assume this is true is not even noticed; let alone questioned.

Self-Inquiry is a very simple technique that acts like a mirror in which instead of assuming we know what we are we are finally able to say "I do not know what this sense of 'I' is". When we are open to actually look and see what this "I" is then we can begin to break down this energetic mass of belief around it. It is almost like melting an iceberg and Self-Inquiry is the heat. Every time we assume we are a person (a mind and a body separate from everything else) we are adding to this iceberg and every time we actually look and see inside what we are then we are allowing it to melt a little (or a lot).

This belief that I am a person with problems and things to transcend and a spiritual journey to go on is simply not true and causes a lot of suffering. Self-Inquiry works best when we openly look inside our being and see if we can identify what we actually are. Amazingly when we search our Being we do not find this "me" that inhabits the body. We find we do not actually know what we are.

The Practice of Self-Inquiry

When we openly search our being without any pre-formed opinions about what we will find, then we come to the amazing fact that we cannot find a "me". This entity that we assumed we were is actually not locatable. We can find a body and a sense of someone being here but we cannot actually find a physical location for this "me". It is a kind of sensing or feeling into your Being, it is not a looking with the physical eyes but simply a non-physical searching. You begin to find that you cannot actually find Yourself!

For most people at first this may bring up some fear and this is normal and ok. Our minds are used to thinking of ourselves as being solid objects and while that may be true for the body it is most certainly not true for "me".

Stop right now as you read this and search what you think of as being you and see if you have any edges, boundaries, any limits. Do not assume anything and just actually look. Look and see what you can find and do not be stopped by fear; the mind is scared of what it does not know but you are not your mind.

Ask yourself "What am I?" or "Who am I?" and see what you find. We are not looking for a thought answer although of course your mind will try to supply one. Keep looking even when your mind tells you an answer and see what is revealed to you.

Turning the Tide of Belief

Each time we look and do not find a separate locatable self that is "me" we are moving ever closer to waking up fully and finally. We have all spent many years assuming that we know what we are and we must confirm what we actually are over and over again. As we look and find nothing tangible we are left with the intangible. As we search for a form we are left with only formlessness. As we look for an object we find only the Subjective sense of Self. As we search for a phenomenon called "me" with a location, position and size we can find only the Noumenon; a total lack of phenomena.

As we look and confirm over and over again we begin to turn around the tide of belief and see that we are not a "thing" called "me" at all. In fact we find we are a "no-thing" and that our truest essence is formless, Subjective, Nothingness or more like empty space. This empty space is sentient, intelligent and awake. All phenomena of thoughts, beliefs, bodies, and solid objects come out of this formlessness.

How Can we Use Self-Inquiry?

We can use Self-Inquiry on its own to take us directly to the Noumenon. What is left when we do not find a solid "me" is something intangible; it is the Noumenon. We can also use self-inquiry to break down very strong beliefs that have a lot of pull magnetically. Certain thoughts and beliefs will appear again and again to show us that we are still believing them and this can interrupt our practice in such moments described in the Stage Two practice. Trigger events can cause a barrage of thoughts and an extremely noisy mind which results in a heightened or strong emotional state when the thoughts are believed.

For example we may be aware that there is only abundance in the universe and that any perceived lack is not really true but that may not be enough when we are deeply feeling the Silence and Peace in our Stage One practice and then we are presented with an unexpected bill that we cannot pay. The mind may immediately begin to present thoughts to us such as "how am I going to pay this?" and "I don't have enough money" and these may be very strong neuropathways which pull our attention away from the Noumenon. As we pay attention to these thoughts we will begin to feel strong emotion from believing these thoughts and it may seem impossible in these moments to begin to feel the Noumenon again. When we believe our thoughts we create that experience for ourselves and in this case it will be lack showing up for us again. This in turn reinforces the neuropathways in our brain that produce a strong emotional response of fear, doubt and frustration again and again. We may feel it is all lost in those moments and we are back to where we started.

Self-Inquiry can help here by looking at the reality of the one that feels it is scared, the one that does not have enough. We begin to notice a lack and feel fear and automatically believe in the sense of "me" that has to find a way out of the problem or the "me" that has to find a way back to Silence. By looking inside ourselves for the sense of "me" we are redirecting the attention back to the source of the problem. Over and over in these trigger events we may notice attention immediately goes to what is happening to this sense of "me" and not to the "me" itself. Self-Inquiry questions the actuality of this "me" and begins to search for it. As we look for it and cannot find an objective sense of "me" then the emotional charge around the thoughts and beliefs here begin to dissipate.

We must use Self-Inquiry not just to make our negative emotions go away but to continue further into the inquiry to begin to undo this energetic mass of belief in this separate person. Each time we look we short cut the process to total freedom as the reality of this separate existence becomes less and less convincing. We can begin to see through this psychosomatic world of suffering that is really just a complex series of interconnected neuropathways in our brain that have been energised by belief.

Every time we assume we are this person having a particular problem, emotion or belief we strengthen these neuropathways and suffer. Every time we question the reality of the one that is suffering we put the egoic sense of self on a countdown timer to its dissolution.

The egoic sense of self is simply a collection of unquestioned beliefs about ourselves. Once the validity of the person has been questioned you can never suffer the same again. Each time you look and do not find the actual separate person it becomes harder and harder to believe it next time.

The first belief we assume to be true is that we are this separate person or that "I am this body". Question this belief by Self-Inquiry and all other beliefs will have no ground to stand on.

CHAPTER 22

The Short Cut

At any point along stage One, Two or Three practice we can use the process of Self-Inquiry to speed up our progress. As we begin to spend more and more time as the Noumenon then we will be able to overcome obstacles easier and easier. Self-Inquiry helps that and at some point it will be seen very clearly that you are NOT an object and you never have been.

You will probably find that Self-Inquiry will begin to happen by itself more and more often as an area where you still believe yourself to be a person shows up for you. The habit before may have been to automatically believe the thoughts and emotions about your beliefs and this is reinforced by memories of experiences where these beliefs seemed to be very true. Quite naturally as you see yourself more and more as the Timeless, Formless One then you will begin to question automatically how real this separate person is in these moments.

The Short Cut Process

There is a way to hasten this process too and you will know when you are ready for this because your attention will be drawn to the questions in this chapter. Suddenly the questions will seem appealing, interesting and even though they may feel a little dangerous to the mind they draw you into them. Before you are ready the questions may seem obvious, irrelevant, boring or even pointless. At some point they will become living questions for you that you take inside your being and allow to do their work.

Waking up fully and living from the Truth always is simply a process of dissolving the energy of separation in the body caused by this belief in you as a separate being. It involves a change in brain chemistry and an openness to see yourself as being the Formlessness that no problem can affect.

The short cut process will help you with this. It is a question that is designed to dissolve the questioner. If the sense of being separate is simply an energetic mass of belief in our mind then these questions will enable clear Seeing to occur which will cut through this energetic mass.

As with Self-Inquiry these questions do not require a mental answer. They are supposed to be living questions that you ask and allow the question to sink deeper into your being. It is almost as if you ask the question and then let it go. Perhaps a mental answer will come or perhaps not but it does not matter.

The Questions:

- **Can the Perceiver be perceived?**
- **Can the Observer be observed?**
- **Can the Seer be seen?**

These questions have powerful catalytic power in them and can help to awaken you. Never underestimate the power of these questions. Pick one that appeals to you and spend some time just looking and being with the question. You can even abandon all attempts to get an answer.

You will become the answer!

Something is observing your thoughts and emotions but can you observe the One observing?

Something is perceiving all this inner and outer world and all that happens in it; but can you perceive this One that is perceiving?

Something is seeing the thoughts, feelings, body, world, events, relationships and everything. Something sees the whole universe. But can the One seeing be seen?

As you ask these questions and allow them to become a living thing inside you then you are asking with your whole Being. These questions are very direct, powerful and a concentrated form of Self-Inquiry.

These questions have the power to end all suffering!

When you feel a pull magnetically to these questions then the end of suffering is near.

What you begin to find is that you cannot be seen, perceived or observed as an object or a phenomenon. You can only see YourSelf as the Noumenon in which all phenomena appear. Over and over it becomes confirmed again and again that you are the Noumenon viewing Itself. You are using time and space and form to perceive the Timeless and Formless One.

CHAPTER 23

Resistance, Obstacles and Distractions Along the Pathway

Our mind has been used to thinking and perceiving the same way for a long time and therefore it WILL put up resistance to this process. To believe it will not or that you are not affected by it is naïve and will delay the process. Mind will produce doubts, worries, fears and seeming roadblocks along the pathway that may seem insurmountable at the time. This book is here to tell you that you can transcend ANY blockage or limitation ultimately by knowing what you are. No thought, emotion, problem or obstacle can stop you from Being what you already are. These obstacles all have a "thing-ness" quality to them and as the Ultimate Seer you are the space in which they are appearing. How much do the objects in the room affect the space in the room? Is it altered in any way if the room is full or empty?

The Key to Moving Beyond Resistance

If we can learn to expect the obstacles to be different every time then we will be better prepared. Learning to look at the obstacles as helping us will allow us to view them more compassionately and dissolve them faster. Your mind is trying to keep things the same as they always have been because it believes that is how to keep you safe. It firmly believes you are a separate being that has a finite beginning and ending and as such is doing everything it does to protect you. The mind has NO ability to see the True Self or the Noumenon because it cannot perceive something that is not an object. The mind is an object (a very subtle one) that is designed, used for and very good at perceiving objects. When we ask the mind to perceive the Subject it cannot and therefore it becomes afraid of what it cannot see or understand. When the mind begins to fear it will resist your efforts to awaken fully.

This does not need to stop you however as compassionate understanding of the mind dissolves it. Understanding WHY your mind is trying to stop you is vital and allows you to view it more as a kind of cute but annoying animal that knows no better.

We cannot expect our mind to be able to perceive That which the mind emerges out of. It would be like asking a movie to understand and comprehend the screen and projector used to view it AND the writer, actors and script. The mind is a set of automatic ways of looking at or thinking about things and as such it is not sentient. It is NOT able to make a decision and say "oh well I understand now and will stop resisting".

We can also begin to look at our mind as our best friend that is going to push us until we develop enough spiritual muscle power to stay as the Noumenon no matter what.

Each time we feel some pattern of thinking and feeling about something is too strong to find the Noumenon then we are forced to look deeper within us for that strength of conviction that must be here. The Noumenon (You) is all things in potential and no thing in actuality yet. This means that it is a Silent, Invisible Field in which the potential exists for everything. It is therefore up to you what potential you make appear into its actuality and these trigger events are there to make you dig deeper and look for the absolute conviction that can only come from the Self and not the self.

No amount of resistance is bigger than You for You have no size. No amount of thoughts about a certain situation is more true than You for You are the Absolute Truth. No mind pattern has more power than You because You are the Infinite Power.

Rather than wondering IF you are resisting the process right now it would be much easier, simpler and MUCH less painful to ask "please show me where I am resisting right now".

Distractions

One of the ways you will see resistance coming to the surface in practical terms is distraction. This is the mind's key way of getting you to lose your focus. It may start in a very simple way such as the thought "I don't have time to sit and tune in to the Noumenon today" or it may be a subtle feeling of restlessness that means you just cannot get comfy in your meditation seat. It may occur as feeling irritable or a sudden urge to sleep.

Most people will feel many distractions occur whilst committed to their stage one and two practice and these range from very earthly methods of distraction to sublime and "spiritual" ones. It would take a whole book in itself to list all the ways you might notice your mind trying to distract you. Everyone's path is unique to them and everyone's way of distracting themselves is unique too. Take a look at which ways you regularly take time for activities that do not need to be done and you will see how you are allowing yourself to be distracted!

Here is a list of common distractions that may happen for you:

1 - Too much bliss during practice. In this situation the amount of bliss becomes seemingly too much and you feel the urge to stop. This can be dealt with by surrendering the bliss to the Noumenon/Divine and all is ok. You are the Field and the bliss is emerging out of it and You remain unaffected.

2 - Sudden urge to fix something. Here the mind can suddenly come up with an idea to get something done, fixed or altered that seems to need to be done urgently. Simply notice that the urge only came when you sat down to meditate and that is no coincidence!

3 - Tiredness. Each one of us will face this distraction at some point. We feel fine and calm and we sit to meditate and suddenly all we can do is yawn and our head begins to nod each time we relax into meditation. Here we can overcome this distraction by again noticing that we did not feel tired before we sat down. Notice also how magically we feel energetic again once we have gone about our business again.

4 - Obsessively watching TV, movies or playing games. Along with this also goes social media and other sites! Notice what you habitually do often without any seeming control of it. Are you constantly glued to your phone?

5 - Fear or some other emotion coming up. In this situation the mind can use many "what if..." questions to elicit fear such as "what if I cannot function and look after my children or work after the ego has dissolved?"

6 - Reading spiritual books. At a certain point reading books such as this is a help to our practice but once

we have seen what we are and have committed to our Stage One practice we may find ourselves reading again as a way to distract ourselves from the Silence. Thinking about Silence is NOT the same as listening for it. Reading about Silence is NOT the same as listening for it and Being it.

7 - Endless questions about the process, the practice or the True Self Itself. No question can show you what you are but some questions can help to clear up doubts or confusions. At a certain point you may notice your mind is simply asking questions to make sure that you feel you need an answer to it before you can wake up fully. Many questions can be ignored once you have seen what you are. If your mind wants to obsessively ask questions then read the list of questions in the "Short Cut" chapter and focus on them.

8 - Feeling as though you need to read one more book, attend one more Satsang or listen to one more teacher before you can wake up. This is simply not true.

9 - Feeling unworthy or not good enough to wake up fully. Again this is simply not true; you are already the Noumenon and need not become it. You only need to recognise this.

10 - Feeling as though you need a live teacher there in front of you. Again this is not needed because the true teacher is within you and if you need a prompt then you will receive this guidance from the heart.

As we have said we cannot have a total list here of all the ways your mind will try to distract you but if you want to see what ways it is trying then you will be shown. A willingness to see is all that is needed.

Common Obstacles

Fear of Not Being Able to Function

This is common to nearly every spiritual student and occurs because our mind or separate sense of self cannot possibly accept or understand that our functioning in the world is due to the True Self right now. We fear how we will move around, go to work, raise our children and live our daily life without a separate sense of self. We live under the illusion that it is this "me" that is making it all happen and making sure we get to work on time or remember to pick up the kids from school.

As we grow and progress in our Stage One and Two practice, we will see that everything is simply happening by itself and if we need to remember something, plan something or use our mind after awakening we will and can thanks to the power of the Noumenon. Our ego was never in charge no matter how much it tried to convince us. We survived and made it into adulthood despite the ego and not because of it!

Amazingly we find the opposite of the fear is true and we are more able to function clearly and efficiently the more awake we are. We can actually listen to others for the first time instead of listening with our own agenda. We can love unconditionally and yet not be taken advantage of. We have more energy and a quiet mind to see exactly what the best course of action is without the stress of trying to decide and weigh the options, which is all the mind can do.

For the first time ever perhaps we find ourselves fully here, present and alive.

Periods Where Nothing Seems to be Happening

If we are serious about wanting to awaken fully we must come to accept now that there will be periods of time in our practice where it appears that nothing is happening. Inside of us and deep down there is a profound change occurring but we may not see it as yet; just as when a seedling grows we see nothing happening for a while as the roots develop under the soil. From that seedling a mighty oak tree will grow and then a whole forest of trees but if we look at this initial stage for results then we may be disappointed. Learn to disregard this need for outer results. The outer world is a world of effects only and has no power. All change comes from within and you will see soon enough. Simply keep focused and stop looking for results.

Too Much Stillness and Bliss

As you move deeper into your practice you may find that Stillness, Silence and Bliss can seem to become very strong at moments. You may even experience strong surges of energy in the body and many other physical experiences. You may have moments that seem overwhelmingly loving and as though you cannot handle all the love. There might be some profound experiences or some awful despair and doubts. There may be dark moments when you seem to have lost your way.

How do we cope with all this and still function and continue? The answer is always to be the Noumenon in which these moments are happening. Surrendering the bliss, doubts, fears, energetic movements or whatever is happening to the Self and staying ONLY as the Noumenon is the answer for all that may seem to occur. It is that simple. You can only struggle with too much bliss if you feel you are the one that is feeling blissful. You can only feel that the Stillness will not allow you to move if you think you are the one moving! Stay as the Awareness only, BE the Noumenon and all will be simple and clear. This surrendering will become automatic for you as you easily choose the Noumenon.

Whatever problem you have along the way MUST be a problem of the ego and not the Noumenon. Make a choice to be only the Noumenon and turn to it whenever you notice your attention has gone back to the sense of "me" and its problems. Do this and watch all issues melt away.

The Power to Ignore

Eventually you will see that you are developing only one skill really and that is the power to ignore thoughts. This does not make thoughts wrong or bad! It is simply that you know where that road goes and you have been down it many times. You know what happens when you listen to your mind.

Developing the power to ignore is as simple as turning attention away and staying with YourSelf. If you were in a busy market place and you were walking through it on your honeymoon all your attention would be on your new husband or wife and you would NOT need to be dragged away from other people.

When a train comes into a station you do not automatically get on it; you wait for the one that takes you where you want to go. Similarly you do not try to get into every car in the car park but you walk only to your car and drive away. This power to ignore is innate in you but you have never used it on thoughts before. Think of everyone you met yesterday as you went through your day. Can you remember every little detail of what they said, how they moved and what they were wearing? Of course not! You have naturally learned to ignore and filter out what is extraneous and not useful. Simply do this with the mind now!

What if you could simply turn away from any thought? What if no thought was appealing because you know how that ends? This power is already with you!

CHAPTER 24

Asking for Help

The irony of waking up is that we come to see that we are all One Consciousness appearing as many and yet somehow we must choose to do the work alone. No Teacher, Sage or Guru can make this happen for you. You must take responsibility for the work by YourSelf and make it happen. Nobody can be in your mind choosing what to focus on in every moment. You must choose as a seemingly separate entity until the chooser has vanished. Each moment you do not make a conscious choice you are unconsciously choosing to stay asleep.

Another ironic thing is that the very moment you choose to do this work then the whole Universe begins to move for you and with you. A multitude of unseen help will come to you in all manner of ways. So you must stand alone and resolute and yet the moment you do then all the Awakened Beings that have ever walked this earth will come to aid you.

No Sage has favourites and they are there to help any genuine spiritual seeker along the way at every step. You need only ask. Some may call this praying but it can be as simple as saying "Help me please". You may feel called to ask that you be absorbed into the Infinite Field of You. You might feel more aligned to surrender everything and yourself to God.

Whichever way you feel the urge to admit you need help then do so. Humility is the key to success and we are never more humble than when we know we don't know what to do.

As a separate person you cannot wake up because you do not exist. You are an apparition in the Totality and as you ask for help then you allow the Field of Infinite Possibility to help you. You allow the Self to help you. You have already tried to do it by will power and effort and it did not work. Nobody ever woke up this way.

Your mind has no idea how to wake up or even what the Awakened State feels or looks like. All it can do is look for feelings or sensations and compare them with previous ones. The Noumenon is not a feeling.

Ego is Arrogance

The ego survives because we think we know what to do or not do or who we are. These are all assumptions that are untrue. A Wise One knows that she does not know and this not knowing brings total peace and clarity. Ask any person you meet who they are and they will probably look at you strangely, as if it is an absurd question because they know they are the "me" or they might tell you their name. Either way it is assumed this name is me and that is all there is to it. Be humble enough to know you do not know and this undoes immediately all the arrogance.

"I know" is close-minded arrogance.

"I don't know" is humility and openness that must lead to awakening.

The Truth is that you do not really know anything. Ask to be shown what each thing means rather than assuming "this is good" or "this is bad".

Aligning With a Master

If you have access to a True Teacher then align with them, ask for their help. Ask for any help you can get. You may feel called to a particular Master such as Christ, Krishna or the Buddha. You may simply feel connected to the Angels or have your own way of receiving help. It does not matter what you call it because you are really finessing the Power of the Infinite Noumenon to help you.

Be open, humble and determined and you HAVE to succeed. It is not a question of if you will wake up but when. All the Sages of ages gone past and present have been through this process and there is no shortcut.

All you need will come to you; simply make the first step. Be devoted to Truth and all else will happen for you step by step.

You can do this. You are already That which you are seeking.

CHAPTER 25

Summary of Common Names for the Noumenon

Below are some of the ways the Noumenon has been described in other teachings. For each set of terms there are two names. Reading through the list may help to awaken a recognition in you as you read and at certain times along the way different sets of terms may be more appealing than others.

They are all names for That Which Has No Name. Don't get attached to any name; look at what the name points to.

NOUMENON	PHENOMENA
Oneness	many
Allness	separation
Empty Mind	full mind
Unity	multiplicity
Silent Mind	noisy mind
Non-Duality	duality
"I" as Consciousness	"I" as a person
Nothingness	somethingness
Awakeness	sleep/dream
Consciousness	unconsciousness

Silence	sound
Subjectivity	object
Being	being someone/something
Stillness	movement
Presence	person
God	ego
Truth	falsehood
Formless	form
Reality	illusion
Knowingness	knowing about
Awareness	perception
Context	content
Infinite Field	finite being
Timeless	duration

If you would like more information about Helen Hamilton, her live Satsangs, silent retreats and classes please contact us:

Our website is www.helenhamilton.org

Find us on facebook by searching @satsangwithhelenhamilton

Search for us on YouTube at "Satsangwithhelenhamilton"

Email us at evolutionofspirit@gmail.com

Printed in Great Britain
by Amazon